A DUBLIN BLOOM

*An original free adaptation
of James Joyce's **Ulysses***

DERMOT BOLGER

New Island Books/ Dublin
Nick Hern Books/ London

A Dublin Bloom

An original free adaptation of James Joyce's *Ulysses*
is first published in June, 1995
in Ireland by
New Island Books,
2, Brookside,
Dundrum Road,
Dublin 14
Ireland

& in Britain by
Nick Hern Books,
14 Larden Road,
London W3 7ST.

ISBN 1 874597 26 X (New Island Books)
1 85459 214 9 (Nick Hern Books)

New Island Books receives financial assistance from
The Arts Council (**An Chomhairle Ealaíon**),
Dublin, Ireland.

Cover design by Jon Berkeley
Typeset by Graphic Resources
Printed in Ireland by Colour Books, Ltd.

Playwright's Note

In 1993 I was approached by Mr Greg Doran, from the Royal Shakespeare Company in London, who had just staged an acclaimed version of *The Odyssey* by Derek Walcott, and now wished for me to do a stage adaptation of *Ulysses*.

Naturally I refused his offer several times, not through any dislike of the novel, but for quite the opposite reason. I genuinely believed it to be an impossible task, and certainly one which I did not feel qualified to undertake. What finally persuaded me to attempt such an undertaking was a realisation that the fear which held me back from trying to adapt the novel was an extension of the fear which holds so many people back from simply reading it. A fear which I increasingly felt had nothing to do with either the book or the author but with an aura which has grown up around *Ulysses*.

In addition to being the greatest novel ever published, *Ulysses* is also among the most intricate and complex. But part of its very greatness is that it is also, on a very basic level, a relatively straightforward account of a quite ordinary (and yet utterly extraordinary) day.

I am no Joyce expert whatsoever, and my response to the book has always been on a very human level. Consequently I have tried to draw as clean a line as possible through the book and, although some liberties needed to be taken for theatricality's sake, I have refused to budge from the book beyond that point. If not a good enough playwright (and I am not quite sure who would be) to bring out the true complexity of such a book on the stage, I hope that perhaps I am a simple enough one to unravel the story of Mr Bloom's day in a manner that may lead at least some people back to the actual reading and enjoyment of the superb novel itself.

I would like to express my thanks to Mr Greg Doran for his support, to Mr Nick Marston in London, to Hazel and Leo Duffy (in whose Victorian house within two hundred yards of Eccles Street this adaptation was written), to Mr Fred Hass and the Hass Charitable Trusts in the U.S.A. who helped the Rosenbach in the commissioning of this work, to everybody in the Rosenbach Museum & Library in

Philadelphia which houses James Joyce's autographed manuscript of *Ulysses* and who commissioned and staged this work (most especially its director, Mr Stephen K. Urice, its Bloomsday Coordinator, Ms Marian Eide, and the co-chairpersons of the Rosenbach Bloomsday Committee, Ms Mary Kelly Doran and Ms Carolyn Payne Langfitt), and especially to Mr Stephen Joyce and the Estate of James Joyce who gave permission for a single American staging on Bloomsday, 1994.

A final and very special thanks must go to the Philadelphia cast and backroom people who put such intense effort and commitment into the success of the production.

Dermot Bolger,
Dublin,
16th of June, 1995

A Dublin Bloom (an original free adaptation for the stage of James Joyce's *Ulysses*) was commissioned by, and received its world premiere from, *The Rosenbach Museum & Library* in celebration of the 90th Bloomsday, on Thursday, 16th of June, 1994 at the Zellerbach Theatre, The Annenberg Center, University of Pennsylvania, Philadelphia, U.S.A.

Director: Greg Doran

Cast: Paul Bernardo
                   Susanne Case
                   Jennifer Childs
                   Robert Gilbo
                   Allison Green
                   Daryll Heysham
                   Michael MacCauley
                   Christine Vanacore
                   Paul Wagar
                   H. Michael Walls

Notes to a Reading of
A Dublin Bloom

A Dublin Bloom has been written for a cast of at least eleven adults, plus one youth and one young girl. The adults (with the exceptions of Leopold Bloom, Molly Bloom and Stephen Dedalus) all play a huge variety of roles. For a clearer reading of this text, however, the keys to these role changes (i.e. "enter Actor A as Cunningham") have been removed, and stage directions reduced to a bare mimimum.

The actors playing Leopold Bloom, Molly Bloom and Stephen Dedalus remain in the same roles throughout. Of the four other actors: ACTOR A plays mainly solid citizen roles (Cunningham, Father Commee, M'Coy, The Veteran, etc), ACTOR B plays what are often rakish roles (Lenehan, Lynch, Lyons, etc), ACTOR C plays Simon Dedalus, and other general roles, while ACTOR D plays mainly "villian" roles (Boylan, Mulligan, The Citizen, etc).

Of the four actresses: ACTRESS A plays mainly mature women (Bella Cohen, etc.), ACTRESS B frequently plays male cameos and also rather worn female roles (Josie Breen, Ellen Bloom, etc.), ACTRESS C plays young roles (Milly Bloom, Dilly Dedalus, Zoe Higgins, Gerty, but also the ghost of Stephen's mother), while ACTRESS D plays mainly younger roles and also some male cameos.

THE GIRL is a waif-like scene setter, but also plays a young whore in Nighttown. THE YOUTH is also used as a sort of urchin-like scene setter but he also plays such vital roles as Rudy Bloom and Patrick Dignan (Junior). THE GIRL and YOUTH are not part of the cast in relation to the chorus, etc. Mainly they serve as walking clothes horses, dispensing costumes and moving about props. They have a tailor's rail of clothes, which they move about the stage as if pulling it through the streets of Dublin.

Where there are two different locations within a particular scene the symbol< > has been used to show the switch in focus. All props and costumes should be kept to the absolute minimum, with effects created mainly by voices, music and lighting.

Below is a full breakdown of all characters and roles:

ACT ONE

ACTOR A plays:

(Prologue)

M'Coy

(Lotuseaters)

M'Coy

(Hades)

Cunningham

(Aeolus)

McHugh,

(Laestrygonians)

A Diner,

(Wandering Rocks)

Fr. Commee,

M'Coy

(Sirens)

Dollard,

(Cyclops)

Bergan

ACTOR B plays

(Prologue)

Lenehan)

(Lotuseaters)

Banton Lyons

(Hades)

Kelleher

(Aeolus)

Lenehan

(Laestrygonians)

Preacher

A Diner

(Wandering Rocks)

Sailor

Lenehan

(Sirens)

Lenehan

(Cyclops)

Bob Doran

ACTOR C plays

(Prologue)

Pub Narrator

(Hades)

Simon Dedalus

(Aeolus)

Simon Dedalus

(Laestrygonians)

A Diner

(Wandering Rocks)

Simon Dedalus

(Sirens)

Simon Dedalus

(Cyclops)

Pub Narrator

ACTOR D plays

(Prologue)

The Citizen

(Telemachus)

Mulligan

(Nestor)

Deasy

(Hades)

Jack Power

(Aeolus)

Tram Inspector

Myles Crawford

(Laestrygonians)

A Diner

(Wandering Rocks)

Boylan

(Sirens)

Boylan

(Cyclops)

The Citizen

ACTRESS A plays

(Prologue)

Martha

(Lotuseaters)

Postmistress

Martha

(Hades)

The Male Mourner

(Wandering Rocks)

The Posh Lady

Boylan's Secretary

(Sirens)

Miss Kennedy

(Cyclops)

Garryowen (the dog)

ACTRESS B plays

(Prologue)

Joe Hynes

(Calypso)

The Cat,

(Hades)

Priest at Funeral,

(Aeolus)

Male Works Manager,

(Laestrygonians)

Josie Breen,

(Sirens)

Miss Douce

(Cyclops)

Joe Hynes

ACTRESS C plays

(Telemachus)

Stephen's Mother's Ghost

(Calypso)

Milly,

(Hades)

Altar Boy,

(Wandering Rocks)

Dilly Dedalus,

(Cyclops)

Jarvey.

ACTRESS D plays

(Lotuseaters)

Lady climbing onto coach

(Hades)

Shawled Mourner

(Laestrygonians)

Waitress,

(Wandering Rocks)

Shop Girl,

Male Bookseller,

ACT TWO

ACTOR A plays

(Nausikaa)
Priest in church
(Circe)
Private Carr,
Groper,
Heckler,
Barrister,
Hangman,
City Coucillor,
Medical Expert,
(Cabman's shelter)
Veteran.

ACTOR B plays

(Nausikaa)
Church Goer
(Oxen of the Sun)
Story-teller
(Circe)
Drunk,
Lynch,
2nd Watch,
Bishop,
Preacher,
Kelleher,
(Cabman's shelter)
Jarvey.

ACTOR C plays

(Nausikaa)
Church Goer,

(Circe)
Idiot,
Cyclist,
Shebeenkeeper,
1st Watch,
Publican,
(Circe)(Cabman's shelter)
Sailor

ACTOR D plays

(Nausikaa)
Church Goer,
(Circe)
Private Compton,
Rudolph Bloom,
Myles Crawford,
Judge,
Hornblower,
Boylan,
(Cabman's shelter)
Shelter keeper

ACTRESSES A plays

(Circe)
Martha,
Rich Woman,
Bella Cohen,
Shawlled Hag,

ACTRESS B plays

(Nausikaa)
Cissy Caffrey,
(Circe)

Ellen Bloom,
Josie Breen,
Dignan's Ghost,
Blacksmith,
Shawlled Woman,
Kitty Rickets,
Male Bidder,
(Cabman's shelter)
Lord John Corley

ACTRESSES C plays

(Nausikaa)
Gerty MacDowell,
(Circe)
Gerty MacDowell,
Mary Driscoll,
Zoe Higgins,
Male Bidder,
Mother's Ghost

ACTRESS D plays

(Nausikaa)
Edy Boardman
(Circe)
Bawd,
Rich Woman,
Rate Payer,
Florry Talbot,
Male Bidder,
(Cabman's shelter)
Haggard Whore.

For Greg Doran

ACT ONE

The stage is divided into three areas by a raised platform at the centre back which has steps leading up. On this platform MOLLY'S bed is integrated on a rake which can be switched front and back, so that she is visible when speaking but the bedstead can be raised in blackout to block her from view.

Gradually MOLLY'S raked bed is highlighted. BLOOM pulls on long white nightshirt, takes pillow and, pulling back blankets, places it at sleeping MOLLY'S feet. He enters bed softly and, head resting on pillow, eases up MOLLY'S nightclothes to kiss both her buttocks. Stage goes to blackout filled by swelling music and voices.

    THE CITIZEN: By Jesus, I'll crucify that bloody jewman, so I will.

    MARTHA: Are you not happy in your home you poor naughty boy?

    M'COY: Who's getting it up? Blazes Boylan?

    REST OF CAST: Trembling calves. Butcher's buckets. Rawhead and bloody bones.

There is a brief strobe of light. The cast stand around bed, palms outstretched as if trying to levitate BLOOM.

    LENEHAN: What's your hurry, Boylan? Got the horn or what?

    ACTRESS A: *(Reciting)*   Her mouth glued on his in a voluptuous kiss...

    PUB NARRATOR: And Bloom's old fellow before him, the robbing bagman that poisoned himself...

    HYNES: A dark horse himself, the same Bloom.

Light strengthens for us to distinguish BLOOM who now kneels centre stage in nightshirt, eyes bereft of expression. The cast are background figures, indistinguishable except for THE BOY (as angelic eleven-year-old RUDY) caught in beam of light behind Bloom, dressed in white period suit, reading from a book which he kisses and smiles. His free hand holds a slim ivory cane. He looks up to watch BLOOM silently, then smiles before walking away to distant echo of hooves and a single carriage passing at funeral pace. Behind him a tiny child's coffin is briefly highlighted before the spotlight dies.

Behind BLOOM, ACTRESSES A and B form the shape of an overcoated figure with hat. The shape breaks as BLOOM turns head slowly. One holds out his hat, one his coat. They beckon him.

BLOOM: Again?

They smile, moving back slightly. He rises, sleepwalking, gaze fixed on actresses drawing him into their dream world.

REST OF CAST: *(Sleepy chant)*   With Sinbad the Sailor and Tinbad the Tailor and Jinbad the Jailor and Whinbad the Whaler round a roc's auk's egg in the night of the bed of all the auks...

ACTRESS B: Dream it all again, Leopold Bloom.

Stage goes to blackout.

< >

A spotlight hits the bed where MOLLY rises on elbow to looks at covered shape (made by pillows) of BLOOM.

MOLLY: YES because he never did a thing like that before - as ask to get his breakfast in bed with a couple of eggs since the City Arms hotel - when he used to be pretending to be laid up to make himself interesting to that old faggot Mrs Riordan - and she never left us a farthing - all for masses for her soul - greatest miser - I suppose she was pious because no man would look at her twice - a wonder she didn't want us to cover our faces...

She glances sharply at sleeping shape of BLOOM.

yes he came somewhere - Im sure by his appetite - anyway love its not or hed be off his feed thinking of her - so either it was one of those night women or else its some little bitch he got in with on the sly - if they only knew him as well as I do - and then the usual kissing my bottom was to hide it...

not that I care two straws who he does it with so long as I dont have the two of them under my nose - like that slut - that Mary Driscoll - we had in Ontario terrace padding out her false bottom to excite him...

yes because he couldn't possibly do without it that long since the last time he came on my bottom - I wonder was Boylan satisfied with me today - one thing I didn't like his slapping me behind going away - though I laughed - Im not a horse am I - I wonder is he awake thinking of me or dreaming - am I in it - anyhow its done now once and for all - why cant you kiss a man without going and marrying him first...

Spot dies, obscuring MOLLY as light returns to BLOOM. He has trousers and shirt on now, but his gaze is still trance-like. ACTRESSES A and B stand either side of him, as guides.

ACTRESS B: Dream it all again, Leopold Bloom.

ACTRESS A: A morning...

ACTRESS B: Yesterday's morning...

ACTRESS A: A distant seascape...

ACTRESS B: Sandycove, the snotgreen sea...

ACTRESS A: The windy parapet of a tower...

ACTRESS B: The voice you could not have heard...

ACTRESS A: Of a son in mourning...

ACTRESS B: Not your son, no son will mourn you.

SCENE ONE

Telemachus. The Tower, Sandycove,   **8 a.m. 16th June, 1904**

The bedsprings jingle, startling BLOOM, whose eyes flicker towards BUCK MULLIGAN who carries a bowl of lather, on which a mirror and razor lie crossed, over to raked bedstead.

MULLIGAN: *(Intoning as he holds bowl aloft)*   Introibo ad altare Dei. *(Calls coarsely)* Come up, Kinch, you fearful jesuit.

STEPHEN DEDALUS joins him at bedstead, voices reaching BLOOM as if in a dream.

MULLIGAN covers the bowl, adding in a preacher's tone:

For this, O dearly beloved, is the genuine Christine: body and soul and blood and onus. Slow music, please. (*Smiles*) The mockery of it. Your absurd name, Dedalus, an ancient Greek.

STEPHEN: Tell me Mulligan. How long is Haines going to stay in the tower?

MULLIGAN: Isn't he dreadful? God, these bloody English. Bursting with money and indigestion. He can't make you out. O, my name for you is the best: Kinch, the knife-blade.

STEPHEN: He was raving all night about shooting a black panther. I'm no hero. If he stays I am off.

Behind BLOOM, ACTRESSES A and B have dropped down to form the image of a panther between them. Mulligan reaches across into Stephen's pocket.

MULLIGAN: Lend us a loan of your noserag. (*Produces a crumpled handkerchief from STEPHEN'S pocket and wipes razorblade*) A new art colour for our Irish poets: snot-green. (*Turns abruptly*) The aunt thinks you killed your mother.

STEPHEN: Someone killed her.

MULLIGAN: You could have knelt down, damn it, Kinch, when your dying mother begged you with her last breath to pray for her. There is something sinister in you.

Behind them, MOTHER'S GHOST appears, wasted looking in shroud, to stand behind STEPHEN, holding a white china bowl. She mimes coughing violently into it. MULLIGAN wipes the blade again.

MULLIGAN: You poor dogsbody. I must give you a shirt and a few noserags. I have a lovely pair of breeks with a hair stripe, grey.

STEPHEN: Thanks. I can't wear them if they are grey.

MULLIGAN: (*Holding up a shaving mirror*) Etiquette is etiquette. He kills his mother but he can't wear grey trousers. (*Begins to laugh, turning mirror towards STEPHEN*) Look at yourself, you dreadful bard.

STEPHEN leans across to peer into it and draws back in shock. It is obvious he has seen MOTHER'S GHOST in it.

MULLIGAN: It's not fair to tease you like that, is it? (*Kindly*) God knows you have more spirit than any of them, Dedalus. What have you up your nose against me? Is it Haines?

STEPHEN: Do you remember the first day I went to your house after my mother's death. Your mother asked who was in your room. You said, *O, it's only Dedalus whose mother is beastly dead.*

MULLIGAN: Did I say that? What harm? You saw only your mother die. I see them pop off every day. To me it's all a mockery and beastly. I didn't mean to offend the memory of your mother.

STEPHEN: What about the offence to me?

MULLIGAN: *(Turning)*   O, an impossible person. Look at the sea. What does it care about offences. Come on down. The English swine wants his morning rashers.

Mulligan vanishes. STEPHEN stares ahead as MOTHER'S breath begins to come in hoarse loud rattles.

STEPHEN: *(Whisper)*   No mother. Let me be and let me live.

Bed jangles, breaking spell. STEPHEN and GHOST retreat. BLOOM turns back to his guides who break from the "panther" image to hold out his hat and coat again.

ACTRESS B: Dream it all again, Leopold Bloom.

He moves forward, this time taking hat and coat.

SCENE TWO

Calypso. Mr Bloom's house, Eccles street,   **8 a.m.**

BLOOM becomes animated as ACTRESS B crouches in cat's shape.

CAT: *(Purring, rubbing against BLOOM'S leg)*   Mkgnao! Mkgnao!

BLOOM bends to scratch her neck, then puts hands on his knees.

BLOOM: *(Mockingly)*   Afraid of the chookchooks. I never saw such a stupid pussens.

CAT: Mrkrgnao!

Bloom gives a saucer of milk to CAT and watches her lap it up.

BLOOM: *(Sight making him hungry)*   Ham and eggs, no. No good eggs with this drouth. *(Musing as he checks for a slip of paper in his hat which he then puts on)* Nutty gizzards, liver sliced fried with crustcrumbs. (*Feels pockets for key, briefly taking out a blackened potato*) Better a pork kidney at Dlugacz's. (*Puts hand on banister, listens, then calls*) I'm going around the corner, Molly. (*Pause*) You don't want anything for breakfast?

The only reply is a soft jingle of springs and sleepy grunt that echoes the CAT'S purring. BLOOM exits.

SCENE THREE

Calypso. Mr and Mrs Bloom's bedroom, Eccles street,   8.30 a.m.

Natural light switches to MOLLY who rouses herself sleepily, setting brasses jangling. BLOOM comes scurrying up the stairs, carrying a breakfast tray, with letters on it.

MOLLY: What a time you were, Poldy! I'm parched. Did you scald the teapot? (*BLOOM nods, putting tray down*) Who are the letters from?

BLOOM: A letter for me from Milly and a card for you. (*Slight change of voice*) And a letter for you. (*Places it on bed and watches for reaction. She ignores it, looking at card*) Do you want the blind up? (*He moves away, light spilling over him onto MOLLY, then he glances round to catch her slipping the letter under pillow and glancing at card.*) That do? (*Carefully*) Who was the letter from?

MOLLY: (*Casually*)   O, Boylan. He's coming at four. He's bringing the programme.

BLOOM: (*Trying not to show emotion*)   What are you singing?

MOLLY: La ci darem and *Love's Old Sweet Song*. (*Sips tea with relish, then points to end of bed*) What time is Dignam's funeral?

BLOOM: (*Eyes following her hand*)   Eleven, I think.

He lifts the leg of her drawers from bed. She shakes her head. He tries a garter looped around a stocking.

MOLLY: No: that book. (*He finds it among her underclothes*) Show me. There's a word I want to ask you. (*She sips tea again, then moves down text with a hairpin*) Here. Met him what. What does that mean?

BLOOM: (*Leaning down to look*)   Metempsychosis?

MOLLY: Yes. Who's he when he's at home?

BLOOM: (*Frowning*)   It's from the Greek. The transmigration of souls.

MOLLY: (*Eyes mocking him*)   O, rocks! Tell us in plain words.

BLOOM smiles, lifting the book from her, reading the title and then a line inside it.

BLOOM: Ruby: The Pride of the Ring. "The monster Maffei desisted and flung his victim from him with an oath." (*Looks at MOLLY*) Did you finish it?

MOLLY: Yes. There's nothing smutty in it. Get me another of Paul de Kock's. Nice name he has.

BLOOM: (*Turning the book over, thinking of a better word*) Reincarnation, that's the word. Some people believe that we go on living in another body after death, that we lived before. (*Sees MOLLY'S quizzical look*) Metempsychosis is what the Greeks called it.

MOLLY still looks puzzled. Her spoon ceases to stir sugar. She inhales through arched nostrils.

MOLLY: There's a smell of burning. Did you leave anything on the fire?

BLOOM: (*In panic*)   The kidney!

He runs to the stairs as lights die on platform.

SCENE FOUR

Telemachus. The bathing place, Sandycove,	8.45 a.m.
Calypso. Mr Bloom's convenience, Eccles street,	8.45 a.m.

MULLIGAN and STEPHEN emerge from different sides of platform, MULLIGAN starting to strip off to the waist.

MULLIGAN: Dedalus, I'm stony. Hurry out to your school kip and bring us back some money. Today the bards must drink and junket. But our swim first. Is it time for your monthly wash, Kinch? (*Calls back to unseen HAINES*) You know, Haines, the unclean bard makes a point of washing once a month.

STEPHEN: (*Sour whisper*) I see little hope of money from him.

MULLIGAN: (*Sighs tragically, his hand on STEPHEN'S arm*) To tell you the God's truth I think you're right. Damn all else the English are good for. (*Searches pocket*) Here's your snotrag. Did you bring the key of the tower?

STEPHEN: I have it.

MULLIGAN: (*Calling back*) You know, Haines, the sacred pint alone can unbind the tongue of Dedalus. (*Begins to sing*)

"I'm the queerest young fellow that ever you heard

My mother's a jew, my father's a bird.

With Joseph the joiner I cannot agree,

So here's to disciples and Calvary..."

During this song BLOOM is revealed at back of stage, sitting on an antiquated toilet reading a magazine which he taps unopened letter against. His innocent song takes over from MULLIGAN.

BLOOM: (*Sings*) "O, Milly Bloom, you are my darling,

You are my looking glass from night to morning..."

CAT once again brushes against BLOOM'S leg. BLOOM looks down.

Miaow yourself. Wait till I'm ready. (*Glances at magazine*) "Our prize titbit. Matcham's Masterstroke. Written by Mr Philip Beaufoy, Playgoer's club, London. Payment at the rate of.... (*Sigh of satisfaction at bowel movement)* Might manage... (*Another pleasured sigh*) ...a sketch for Titbits. By Mr and Mrs L. M. Bloom. (*Looks around for paper, then tears off page*) Useful masterstroke.

He turns attention to envelope which he slits open to read as MILLY BLOOM caught in light begins to recite.

MILLY: Dearest Papli, Thanks ever so much for the lovely birthday present. Everyone says I'm quite the belle of Mullingar in my new tam.

BLOOM: (*To himself*)   Fifteen already. First birthday away from home.

MILLY: I am getting on swimming in the photo business now. Mr Coghlan took one of me yesterday and Mrs will send when developed.

BLOOM: Remember the morning she was born, running to knock up Mrs Thornton. Jolly old woman. She knew little Rudy wouldn't live. He'd be eleven now.

<>

MULLIGAN unfreezes, unlacing boots, calling back to STEPHEN.

MULLIGAN: Got a card from Bannon in Mullingar, Dedalus. Says he found a sweet young thing down there. Photo girl he calls her.

<>

MILLY: A student comes here some evenings named Bannon he sings Boylan's song about seaside girls. Tell him silly Milly sends my best respects. Must now close with fondest love. Your fond daughter.

BLOOM: (*Pained*)   Boylan.

<>

MULLIGAN: (*Turning to STEPHEN*)   Give me the key of the tower, Kinch, to keep my chemise flat. (*STEPHEN hesitates*) The key. (*STEPHEN hands it to him*) And twopence for a pint until the school pay you. Throw it there.

MULLIGAN rises, kicking off boots, ignoring STEPHEN who throws pennies down. He runs forward as if into the sea and freezes.

<>

BLOOM: Milly (*Smiles and sings to himself*)
      "All dimpled cheeks and curls...

Your head it simply swirls.

Those girls, those girls..."

(Stops. Humour gone.) Blazes Boylon. His song.

Distant church bells toll. Light becomes more sombre. BLOOM hurries himself.

Quarter to. Late for the funeral. Poor Dignam!

<>

STEPHEN turns to sees MOTHER'S GHOST, wasted hands outstretched.

STEPHEN: I will not sleep here tonight. Home also I cannot go.

Bell tolls loudly, plunging stage into blackness.

SCENE FIVE

Penelope. Molly's bed,   **2 a.m.   (Morning of the 17th)**

Blackout is broken by white spot on MOLLY in the re-raked bed.

MOLLY: yes because the day before yesterday he was scribbling something when I came in to show him Dignams death in the paper - and he covered it up - so very probably that was it to somebody who thinks she has a softy in him - because all men get a bit like that - especially getting on to forty he is now - so as to wheedle any money she can out of him

if they only knew him as well as I do but of course hes not natural - begging me before we got engaged to give him a tiny bit cut off my drawers - till I promised to give him the pair off my doll to carry about - of course hes mad on the subject of drawers - always skeezing at those brazenfaced things on the bicycles with their skirts blowing up to their navels

O Maria Santissima he did look a fool dreeping in the rain that day - beseeching me to lift the orange petticoat I had on - he said had kneel down if I didnt - he would too and ruin his new raincoat - you never know what freak theyd take alone with you - so I lifted them a bit and touched his trousers outside - to keep him from doing worse where it was too public - I was dying to find out was he circumcised - he was shaking like a jelly - they want to do everything too quick - take all the pleasure out of it - then he wrote me that letter - how could he face any woman after - when we met asking me have I offended you - of course he saw I wasnt - then writing a letter every morning - he knew the way to take a woman - then the night he kissed my heart at Dolphins barn - I couldnt describe it - simply it makes you feel like nothing on earth - but he never knew how to embrace well like Gardner in Gibraltar

Spotlight dies, bed raked back in momentary blackout.

SCENE SIX

Lotuseaters. Westland Row post office and environs,   9.45 a.m.

Lights come up. BLOOM removes his hat, wipes brow, quickly takes card from inside hat, glances at it and transfers it to his waistcoat pocket. He takes a folded "Freeman's Journal" from pocket and uses it like a baton as he crosses to bedstead as if it were a grille. He takes out card and hands it in to POST MISTRESS behind the bedstead.

BLOOM: The name is Flower. Henry Flower. Are there any letters for me?

In stylised movement she rises, lifting skirt to remove letter from her garter.

POST MISTRESS: (*Handing letter through bedstead*)   Henry Flower, Esq. C/O Westland Row Post Office?

BLOOM: Thank you. (*Turns, ripping enevlope open, feeling contents carefully*) A photo? No, a badge? (*Looks up, sees M'COY approach and puts letter away, cursing under his breath*) M'Coy. Get rid of him quickly. (*Louder, more jovial*) M'Coy.

M'COY: Hello Bloom... no trouble I hope? I see you're in mourning...

BLOOM: O no. Poor Dignan, you know. The funeral is today.

MARTHA rises as BLOOM fingers letter in pocket.

MARTHA: Dear Henry, I am sorry you did not like my last letter. Why did you enclose the stamps? I wish I could punish you for that.

HAUGHTY WOMAN behind M'COY distracts BLOOM as M'COY speaks. She lifts her skirt, ascending platform as if onto a coach.

M'COY: (*Voice fading as BLOOM'S thoughts take over*)   Poor Dignan. I only heard it last night. Down there in Conway's we were, with Bob Doran on one of his periodical bends, and he said: *Sad thing about our friend, poor little Paddy Dignam. What's wrong with him?* I said. *What's wrong with him. He's dead...*

BLOOM: (*To himself over M'COY'S voice*) Proud: rich: silk stockings. Like that haughty creature at the polo match. Women all for caste till you touch the spot. (*Trying to see round shifting M'COY*) Watch! Silk flash rich stockings white. Watch!

M'COY: (*Voice loud again, attracting BLOOM's attention*) ...and faith, he filled up.

BLOOM tries to shift position but HAUGHTY WOMAN vanishes up onto platform with last flash of white silk stockings.

BLOOM: (*To himself*) Lost her. Curse your noisy pughole. (*To M'COY with sigh*) Yes, yes. Another gone.

M'COY: One of the best. Wife well, I suppose.

MARTHA: Are you not happy in your home you poor naughty boy. I do wish I could do something for you. Dear Henry, when will we meet? I have never felt myself so much drawn to a man as you.

BLOOM: (*Unrolling paper idly to glance at it*) O yes. Tiptop, thanks.

M'COY: My missus has just got an engagement.

BLOOM: (*To himself*) Squealing cat. (*To M'COY, quietly putting him in his place*) My wife too, M'Coy. She's going to sing at a swagger affair in the Ulster Hall, Belfast.

M'COY: (*Impressed*) That so? Who's getting it up?

BLOOM: (*Carefully*) There's a committee formed.

M'COY: (*Nodding*) That's good news. You might just shove my name down at the funeral. I'd go if I possibly could.

BLOOM watches him go and slowly takes the letter out, removing from it a flower on a pin.

BLOOM: No, it's a flower.

He reads carefully, joyfully, then carefully tears the flower from the pin and puts it in his heart pocket.

MARTHA: Please write me a long letter or I will punish you. O how I long to meet you, Henry dear. Goodby now, naughty darling and write by return to your longing MARTHA.

BLOOM: Might be other answers lying in The Irish Times. O, leave them to simmer. Enough bother wading through forty-four replies.

MARTHA: Meet some Sunday after the rosary.

BLOOM: Doing the indignant, respectable character and then the other thing on the sly. A flower. I'll go harder next time.

BLOOM turns, twirling newspaper happily and sees BANTOM LYONS approaching.

LYONS: Hello, Bloom. Show us a minute. (*Reaches for paper*) I want to see about that French horse that's running today.

BLOOM: Ah, Lyons. You can keep it.

LYONS: Ascot. Gold Cup. Half a mo.

BLOOM: I was going to throw it away.

LYONS: (*Looking up, surprised, his voice sharp*) What's that? *Throwaway?*

BLOOM: I said I was going to throw it away, Lyons.

LYONS looks doubtful, then leers, thrusting the paper back at BLOOM with a nod.

LYONS: (*Rushing off*) Throwaway? I'll risk it. Here, thanks.

BLOOM: (*Looking after him in confused amusement*) Lyons shaved off his moustache again to look younger. Dandruff on his shoulders. Scalp wants oiling.

MARTHA: (*Drawing him back into his inner world*) P.S. Do tell me what kind of perfume does your wife use.

BLOOM: Better get that lotion for Molly made up. Where is this? Sweny's in Lincoln Place. Have the chemist make it up and call for it later. And soap. Then time for a bath...

ACTRESSES: (*Gathering behind him*) Gentle tepid steam in the womb of warmth, oiled by scented melting soap, riprippled over, lemonyellow, a languid floating flower.

He begins to lean back as if sinking into a bath when they speak, and they take his weight, rocking him slightly, lulling him, his arms folded across his chest, half lit, Christ-like, being drawn slowly to back of stage.

BLOOM: (*Blissfully looking down as if in blessing*) This is my body.

SCENE SEVEN

Nestor. Mr Deasy's school, Dalkey,   **9.45 a.m.**

As BLOOM lolls in ACTRESSES' arms, forming shape vaguely reminiscent of a crucifixion, STEPHEN moves across the stage to be confronted by MR DEASY.

DEASY: Order restored among the boys on the hockey pitch. Now our little financial settlement, Mr Dedalus.

He slaps open a bound pocketbook and removes two notes which he places in front of STEPHEN.

Two.

He puts pocketbook away and wrestles with moneybox. STEPHEN looks slightly embarrassed as he reaches for the money, watched carefully by DEASY.

Three... three twelve. I think you'll find that right.

STEPHEN: Thank you, Mr Deasy.

DEASY: No thanks at all. Teaching is hard work. Don't carry it like that. Buy one of these machines.

STEPHEN: Mine would be often empty.

DEASY: (*Pointing finger*) Because you don't save. Money is power, if youth only knew. Do you know what is the pride of the English? *I paid my way.* Can you feel that, Mr Dedalus? *I owe nothing.*

STEPHEN: For the moment, no.

DEASY: (*laughing with delight, puting away moneybox*) I knew you couldn't, but one day you must. (*Seriously*) You think me an old fogey, but I remember the famine. We are all Irish, all kings' sons.

STEPHEN: Alas.

DEASY: That reminds me, you can do me a favour with some of your literary friends. I have a letter here. (*He hands STEPHEN some typed sheets, urging STEPHEN to read them*) I have put the matter in a nutshell. It's about the foot and mouth disease. I don't mince words, do I? At the next outbreak they will put an embargo on Irish cattle. I'm going to try publicity. I am surrounded by intrigues, by... (*Raises finger to beat air oldly*) Mark my words, Mr Dedalus. England is in the hands of the Jews. In all the highest places: her finance, her press. Wherever they gather the jew merchants eat up the nation's vital strength. Old England is dying.

STEPHEN: A merchant is one who buys cheaply and sells dear, jew or gentile, is he not?

DEASY: (*Gravely*) They sinned against the light. And that is why they are wanderers on the earth to this day.

STEPHEN: Who has not sinned?

DEASY: What do you mean?

STEPHEN: History is a nightmare from which I am trying to awake.

DEASY: The ways of the creator are not our own.

ACTORS suddenly shout like boys on a hockey pitch.

STEPHEN: (*Jerking thumb towards noise*) That is God.

DEASY: What?

STEPHEN: (*Shrugs his shoulder*) A shout in the street.

DEASY: I foresee that you will not remain long at this work. You were not born to be a teacher.

STEPHEN: A learner rather. (*He rustles sheets*) I will try with these. I know two editors slightly. Good morning, Sir.

STEPHEN begins to walk away but is followed by DEASY.

DEASY: (*Slightly breathless*) Mr Dedalus. Just one moment.

STEPHEN: (*Turning*) Yes sir.

DEASY: Ireland, they say, has the honour of being the only country which has never persecuted the jews. And do you know why?

STEPHEN: Why, sir?

DEASY: (*Solemnly*) Because she never let them in. (*His huge laugh is mixed with a rasping cough. He turns away, hands waving in the air, still laughing*) She never let them in. That's why.

Fade to blackout.

SCENE EIGHT

Penelope. Molly's bed,   **2 a.m. (17th June)**

Blackout broken by white spot on MOLLY.

MOLLY: yes they were all in great style this morning at the grand funeral in the paper Boylan brought in - if they saw a real officers funeral thatd be something - L Bloom and Tom Kernan that drunken little barrelly man and Martin Cunningham and the two Dedaluses - and they call that friendship - killing and burying one another - theyre a nice lot - well theyre not going to get my husband again into their clutches if I can help it - then making fun of him behind his back - poor Paddy Dignam all the same - what are his wife and 5 children going to do - comical little teetotum always stuck up in some pub corner - and Fanny M'Coy - skinny thing with a turn in her eye - trying to sing my songs - and her old green dress with the low neck as she cant attract them any other way - and them others - Kathleen Kearney and her lot of squealers - sparrowfarts skitting around - Irish homemade beauties - theyd die down dead if ever they got a chance of walking in Gibraltar on an officers arm like me - they havent passion God help their poor head - I knew more about men and life when I was 15 than theyll all know at 50 - let them get a husband first thats fit to be looked at and a daughter like mine - or see if they can excite a swell with money that can pick and choose whoever he wants like Boylan to do it 4 or 5 times locked in each others arms (*Look at shape of BLOOM*) - I could have been a prima donna only I married him

Spotlight dies on MOLLY.

SCENE NINE

Proteus. Sandymount Strand,   **11 a.m.**

Greenish light rises on STEPHEN at front of stage. His eyes are closed. He taps with an ashplant.

STEPHEN: (*Low voice*)   Hear your boots crunch, crackling wrack and shells. Signatures of all things I am here to read, seaspawn and seawrack, the nearing tide. Am I walking into eternity along Sandymount Strand? Open your eyes now. Has all vanished since?

(*Opens eyes to look around*) See now. There all the time without you: and ever shall be, world without end. (*Walks forward*) By the way go easy with that money. Yes, I must. So far from Paris. You were going to do wonders, what? A blue French telegram - Mother dying come home father. (*Stops*) Here, turn back. He has the key of the tower. I will not sleep there when this night comes. After Haines woke me last night same dream or was it? Wait. Open hallway. Street of harlots. Remember. That man led me, spoke. I was not afraid.

SCENE TEN

**Hades. Journey from
Sandymount to Glasnevin Cemetery,**   **11 a.m.**

STEPHEN remains frozen as top of stage is lit. BLOOM stands with MARTIN CUNNINGHAM, JACK POWER and SIMON DEDALUS, all dressed for funeral. CUNNINGHAM carefully climbs up the platform and seats himself by kneeling on the bed, while POWER carefully follows him.

POWER: (*Calling back*)   Come on, Simon Dedalus.

BLOOM: (*Standing back for DEDALUS*)   After you.

DEDALUS: (*Climbing up, ignoring BLOOM*)   Yes, yes, Jack.

CUNNINGHAM: Are we all here now? Come on, Bloom.

BLOOM climbs up. All four face the audience, waiting in silence before they begin to sway back and forth slightly.

POWER: Which way is Corny Kelleher taking us, Cunningham?

CUNNINGHAM: Irishtown, Ringsend. Brunswick street.

BLOOM gazes towards STEPHEN who begins to walk off.

BLOOM: There's a friend of yours gone by on Sandymount Strand, Dedalus.

DEDALUS: Who is that?

BLOOM: Your son and heir.

The carriage lurches as DEDALUS leans forward.

DEDALUS: Was that Mulligan cad with him?

BLOOM: No. He was alone.

DEDALUS: (*Snarling*) He's in with a lowdown crowd. That Mulligan is a contaminated doubledyed ruffian by all accounts. But I'll tickle his catastrophe, believe you me. I won't have that bastard ruin my son.

DEDALUS ceases abruptly and leans back. BLOOM closes his eyes a moment, then looks out again to where STEPHEN has vanished.

BLOOM: (*To himself*) Full of his son. He is right. If little Rudy had lived. Something to hand on. My son. Me in his eyes. Strange feeling it would be. Must have been that morning, she at the window watching two dogs at it.

MOLLY'S VOICE: Give us a touch, Poldy. God, I'm dying for it.

BLOOM: (*To himself*) How life begins.

CUNNINGHAM begins to brush the imaginary seat below him.

CUNNINGHAM: (*Breaking BLOOM'S thoughts*) What is this in the name of God, Jack? Crumbs?

POWER: Someone seems to have been having a picnic party here lately.

All raise their thighs, eyeing with disfavour the seats. They jerk as carriage halts.

CUNNINGHAM: What's wrong? We've stopped.

BLOOM: (*Leaning head out*) The Grand Canal. (*Drawing his head back*) The weather is changing.

They lurch forward again.

DEDALUS: It's as uncertain as a child's bottom.

They sit back in silence. CUNNINGHAM leans forward.

CUNNINGHAM: (*Raising palm in salute*) How do you do?

POWER: (*Looking out*) He doesn't see us.

DEDALUS: Who's that, Jack?

POWER: Blazes Boylan. There he is airing his quiff.

BLOOM leans forward, then looks down, examining his nails.

How is the concert tour getting on, Bloom? Are you going yourself?

BLOOM: Well no. In point of fact I have to go down to county Clare on some private business.

POWER: Have you good artists?

BLOOM: O yes, all topnobbers. The best in fact.

POWER: (*Smiling*)   And *Madame* Bloom.

BLOOM unclasps his hands politely, exchanging a smile with POWER. All are relaxed.

CUNNINGHAM: (*Remembering where they are*)   I suppose we had better look a little serious.

DEDALUS: And then indeed poor little Paddy Dignam wouldn't grudge us a laugh, Martin. Many a good one he told himself.

POWER: He had a sudden death, poor fellow.

BLOOM: The best death. (*All turn to observe him*) No suffering. Like dying in sleep.

All are silent. CUNNINGHAM stares out.

CUNNINGHAM: Look! A child's funeral. Sad. In the midst of life.

They look. A BLACK CLOAKED WOMAN passes followed by DAUGHTER.

DEDALUS: Poor little thing. It's well out of it.

POWER: But the worse of all is the man who takes his own life.

CUNNINGHAM, trying to cut POWER off, pulls out his watch briskly, coughs loudly and puts it back again.

The greatest disgrace to have in a family.

CUNNINGHAM: (*Decisively*)   Temporary insanity, of course. We must take a charitable view of it.

DEDALUS: They say the man who does it is a coward.

CUNNINGHAM: It is not for us to judge.

BLOOM seems about to speak, then closes his lips again. His father's distorted voice merges with soundtrack.

FATHER'S VOICE: For my son, Leopold... no more pain... wake no more... nobody owes... my son...

Backdrop throws up shadows of gravestones. All lean to one side as if carriage was swerving in, then jerk a last time as it stops. They climb stiffly down. BLACK CLOAKED WOMAN passes, her DAUGHTER holding her arms out, as if awaiting a sign to cry.

DEDALUS: Here's poor Paddy's coffin now.

CORNY KELLEHER, in undertaker's hat, moves forward, carrying a wreath. BOY (dressed as Dignam's son) also carrying a wreath, is behind him.

DEDALUS: (*Sad dignity*) Corny Kelleher. I am come to pay you another visit so soon.

KELLEHER: (*low voice*) My dear Simon Dedalus, I don't want your custom at all.

He bows and turns with BOY, walking in possession. DEDALUS and BLOOM follow. CUNNINGHAM walks with POWER.

CUNNINGHAM: (*Whisper*) I was in mortal agony with you talking of suicide before Bloom. His father poisoned himself. Had the Queen's hotel in Ennis. You heard him say he was going to Clare. Anniversary.

POWER: O God! First I heard of it, Martin. Poisoned himself.

He glances towards BLOOM. KELLEHER has taken the wreath from BOY and places both wreaths against side of platform. He motions for BOY to kneel. All follow suit. BLOOM waits till others have knelt, then takes out paper and places his knee upon it. PRIEST and ALTARBOY emerge, sprinkling holy water.

PRIEST: Non intres in judicium cum servo tuo, Domine.

BLOOM: (*To himself as others pray*) Makes them feel important to be prayed over in Latin. Father Coffey, with a belly on him like a poisoned pup. What swells him up that way? Molly gets swelled after cabbage. Air of this place maybe? Must be an infernal lot of bad air around. He must be fed up shaking holy water over all the corpses they trot up. Every mortal day a fresh batch: middleaged men, children, women dead in childbirth, consumptive girls with little sparrow's breasts. Says Dignan is going to paradise. Says that over everyone. But he has to say something. Over now. (*Feels pocket*) Where did I put her letter after I read it in the bath?

Others rise and wait until PRIEST, ALTAR BOY and then BOY and KELLEHER pass, before following. DEDALUS, beside POWER, stares to his left, momentarily overcome.

DEDALUS: Her grave is over there. I'll soon be stretched beside her.

POWER: (*Kindly, taking his arm*) She's better where she is, Simon Dedalus.

KELLEHER has stepped aside and stands beside BLOOM.

KELLEHER: (*Politely*) Sad occasions. The others are putting on their hats. We are the last.

They cover their heads as MOURNER (in slightly crumpled bowler) joins POWER.

MOURNER: Who is that chap with the undertaker? I know his face.

POWER: Bloom. Madam Marion Tweedy, the soprano. She's his wife.

MOURNER: O, to be sure. She was a finelooking woman. I danced with her, wait, fifteen, seventeen golden years ago. And a good armful she was. What does he do? Wasn't he in the stationery line?

POWER: (*Smiles*) A traveller for blotting paper. He does some canvassing now for ads for *The Freeman*.

MOURNER: In God's name, what did she marry a coon like that for?

The MOURNER throws up his eyes as BLOOM and KELLEHER reach CUNNINGHAM and DEDALUS.

KELLEHER: They tell the story that two drunks came out here one foggy evening and found the grave of a friend. One of the drunks spelt out the name: Terence Mulcahy. The other drunk is blinking up at a statue of our Saviour the widow had got up. "Not a bloody bit like the man," says he. "That's not Mulcahy, whoever done it."

He is rewarded with smiles all around as he backs away.

CUNNINGHAM: (*Generally*) That's all done to cheer a fellow up. (*To BLOOM*) Bloom, will you come round with me to the widow's house tonight about the insurance? I'll meet you at Barney Kieran's, say at five.

BLOOM nods his agreement as POWER and MOURNER pass them.

BLOOM: Excuse me, sir. (*MOURNER stops.*) Your hat is a little crushed.

MOURNER stares at BLOOM before taking off hat and bulging out the dinge. He clasps hat back on, and jerks his head down.

MOURNER: (*Savagely cutting*) Thank you.

He walks on with the others. Chapfallen, BLOOM drops back and looks after them alone.

BLOOM: How grand we are this morning.

Fade to blackout over sound of grave being filled in.

SCENE ELEVEN

Penelope. Molly's bed,   **2 a.m. (17th June)**

*Spotlight picks up MOLLY more softly. She looks with annoyance at the
sleeping shape.*

MOLLY: I wish he'd sleep by himself with his cold feet - give us
room even to let a fart God or do the least thing - better yes - piano
quietly sweeeee - theres that train far away - pianissimo eeeeeeee -
one more song - that was a relief wherever you be let your wind go
free - (*Looks around*) God here we are as bad as ever after 16 years
- how many houses were we in at all - Raymond terrace and Ontario
terrace and Lombard street and Holles street - and he goes about
whistling every time were on the run again - pretending to help the
man with our 4 sticks of furniture

I dont like being alone in this big barracks at night - the night I was
sure I heard burglars and he went down with a candle and a poker as
if looking for a mouse - making as much noise at he possibly could -
there isnt much to steal indeed the Lord knows - still its the feeling
especially now with Milly away - a musical academy he was going
to make with a brass plate - or Blooms private hotel he suggested -
go and ruin himself altogether the way his father did in Ennis - like
all the things he told father he was going to do but I saw through him
either hes going to be run into prison over his old lottery tickets that
were to be all our salvations - or he goes and gives impudence - well
have him coming home with the sack soon out of the newspaper too
- like the rest - on account of those Sinner Fein or the Freemasons

SCENE TWELVE

Aeolus. Office of The Freeman's Journal,   **12 noon**

*Spot fades on MOLLY. Lighting crosses stage like sheets off a printing
press, the backing track filled with clanking points and huffing trams.
TRAM INSPECTOR briefly takes centre stage.*

TRAM INSPECTOR: (*Calling*) Nelson's pillar, all passengers
dismount. Start, Palmerston Park tram. Rathgar and Terenure tram
starting now. Kingstown and Dalkey. Ringsend and Sandymount
Tower.

NEWSBOY: (*Up on platform*) Press, press! Meet the gentlemen of the press! See Bloom, the canvasser, at work!

At back of stage, CAST (not involved in scene) move in linking mechanical jerks, creating a merging babble of machine noises — "Thumpit-thumpit-thump!", "sllt-sllt-sllt", "clankit-clankit", hell-of-a-racket-hell-of-a-racket" — as BLOOM approaches WORKS MANAGER (obscured by proof-readers cap) who reads an extraordinarily long galleypage. BLOOM holds a square of paper before him.

BLOOM: (*Shouting over noise*) This ad, you see. Alexander Keyes. Tea, wine and spirit merchant. You remember. He wants two crossed keys at the top. Like that. (*Crosses forefingers*) Then the name, Alexander Keyes. Catches the eye, you see.

NEWSBOY: The House of Keyes.

MANAGER: (*Scratching armpit*) Have you the design?

BLOOM: I can get it. But he would need just a little par in the paper calling attention to his shop. You know the usual. High class licensed premises.

MANAGER: (*Turns back to galleypage, ignoring BLOOM*) We can do that. Let him give us a three months renewal.

NEWSBOY: Difficult Assignment for Bloom.

BLOOM: Three months. I'll try. Horseshow month.

BLOOM turns, stops, feeling pocket. Noises momentarily die.

MARTHA'S VOICE: What perfume does your wife use?

BLOOM takes out the soap, smells it, then places it in a different pocket. Printing noises resume.

BLOOM: (*To himself*) Four o'clock Boylan's coming. I could go home still, something I forgot. No.

BLOOM crosses to where MacHUGH and SIMON DEDALUS (holding up a newspaper) stand in a tight arc of light into which the others will have to crowd. Printing noises fade.

NEWSBOY: Editoral Collision Predicted!

As BLOOM enters this arc of light he is hit by LENEHAN arriving behind him.

BLOOM: (*Moving aside*)   I beg yours.

LENEHAN: (*Ignoring BLOOM*)   How was the funeral, Dedalus? (*To MacHUGH*) Is the editor to be seen?

MacHUGH: The very man behind you, Lenehan. Myles Crawford, esq., the sham squire himself.

All look back as MYLES CRAWFORD pushes his way into centre of light.

CRAWFORD: (*Somewhat drunk*)   Getououtthat, you bloody old pedagogue!

DEDALUS: (*Putting on hat*)   I need a drink after that. Will you join me, Myles?

CRAWFORD: Drink! No drink served before Mass, Dedalus.

As DEDALUS exits with momentary upsurge in printing noises. BLOOM, ignored, crosses to back of stage.

BLOOM: (Passing Crawford) I just want to phone Mr Keyes about an ad, Mr Crawford.

LENEHAN: Who wants a dead cert for the Gold cup? *Sceptre.*

NEWSBOY jumps down amongst them, with an upsurge of noise, leaving LENEHAN crestfallen as attention shifts from him.

NEWSBOY: (*Scrambling up*)   It wasn't me, sir. It was the big fellow shoved me, sir.

MacHUGH: (*Throwing NEWSBOY out, noise fading*)   Out of this office with you!

BLOOM: (*Miming holding phone*)   Is the boss... which auction rooms?... Aha! I see... Right...

BLOOM turns, bumping into MacHUGH this time, who grimaces.

MacHUGH: (*Gasp, mock voice*)   "Pardon, memsieur."

BLOOM: My fault. Are you hurt? (*He addresses room*) I'm just running around to Bachelor's Walk about this ad for Keyes's. They tell me he's around there.

CRAWFORD: (*Stretching forth arm*)   Begone! The World is before you.

As BLOOM shuffles quickly away, with upsurge and fade of noise,(as if the door had opened and closed) NEWSBOY mockingly impersonates his walk.

MacHUGH: (*As if peering through window*) Look at the young guttersnipes of newsboys behind him hue and cry. Taking off Bloom's flat spaugs and the walk.

He shuffles in swift caricature towards LENEHAN.

CRAWFORD: (*Snapping to attention*) Where's Simon Dedalus gone?

MacHUGH: The Oval for a drink.

CRAWFORD: Come on then. Where's my hat?

He walks in a jerky circle, loudly fingering his keys.

MacHUGH: (*Whisper*) He's pretty well on, Lenehan.

LENEHAN: (*Offering MacHUGH cigarette*) Seems to be... I was hoping... maybe, he might...

CRAWFORD approaches them, straw hat awry on brow.

LENEHAN: (*Offering CRAWFORD cigarette*) Silence for my brandnew riddle!

As CRAWFORD takes it STEPHEN enters, again with an upsurge and fade of noise, holding typed sheets.

McHUGH: Entrez, mes enfants. Youth visits Notoriety.

CRAWFORD: (*Holding out welcoming hand*) Come in, Stephen. Your governor is just gone.

LENEHAN: (*Trying to get attention back*) Silence. What opera resembles a railway line?

STEPHEN hands sheets to CRAWFORD.

MacHUGH: (*Reading over CRAWFORD's shoulder*) Good day, Stephen. (*Surprised*) Foot and mouth disease.

STEPHEN: The letter is not mine. Mr Garrett Deasy asked me to...

CRAWFORD: That old pelters. I know him, and know his wife too. The bloodiest old tartar God ever made. By Jesus, she had the foot and mouth disease and no mistake. (*Cramming sheets into pocket*) That'll be all right. I'll read the rest after.

LENEHAN: (*Extending hands in protest*) My riddle. What opera is like a railway line? The Rose of Castille. See the wheeze. Rows of cast steel.

He pokes MacHUGH who feigns a gasp. CAST make telephone ringing noise.

MacHUGH: Help. I feel a strong weakness. (*Turns, stylised hand movement*) Hello? Who's there... Yes... (*Covers phone. To CRAWFORD*) It's Bloom.

CRAWFORD: Tell him to go to hell.

MacHUGH: (*uncovering phone, quietly*) Hello Bloom?... Yes, he's still here. Come across yourself.

CRAWFORD: (*Hand on STEPHEN'S shoulder*) I want you to write something for me. Foot and Mouth disease! All balls! Something with a bite in it. Put us all into it, damn its soul. Father Son and Holy Ghost and Jakes M'Carthy.

STEPHEN stares into his drunken eyes. CRAWFORD retreats, jangling keys again.

LENEHAN: (*Quietly*) He wants you for the pressgang. (*After CRAWFORD*) Myles, just one moment. (*Voice fades*). I was wondering if...

NEWSBOY: Gentlemen of the turf hopeful!

CRAWFORD shakes his head to LENEHAN, then returns to STEPHEN, clenching his hand in emphasis.

CRAWFORD: (*To STEPHEN*) You can do it. Something with bite. What do you say?

STEPHEN: (*Discreetly checks pocket*) Gentlemen, may I suggest that the house do now adjourn.

LENEHAN: (*Slightly bitterly*) All who are in favour say Ay. To which particular boosing shed?

CRAWFORD: (*Slapping STEPHEN on shoulder*) Chip off the old block! Let us go. Where are those blasted keys?

NEWSBOY: Return of Bloom!

BLOOM rushes back on stage holding press cutting, followed by mocking NEWSBOY as CRAWFORD turns. Noise resumes fully.

BLOOM: Mr Crawford! A moment! Keyes. (*Crawford looks at him*) He practically promised a renewal for two months. But he just wants a little puff... What will I tell him?

CRAWFORD: (*Throwing arms up for emphasis*) He can kiss my royal Irish arse. Any time he likes. Tell him that straight from the stable. (*Still looking for keys, pulls out letter as he exits*) Foot and mouth. That'll go in.

LENEHAN: (*Bitterly to STEPHEN*) I hope you will live to see it published.

MacHUGH: (*To LENEHAN*) He gave you no hope of a loan so?

LENEHAN: (*Quietly*) Hope. In this place?

All exit, leaving BLOOM behind.

BLOOM: All off for a drink. Arm in arm. Usual blarney. (*Worried*) Wonder is that young Dedalus the moving spirit. Dangerous company.

NEWSBOY: K.M.A. Kiss my Arse.

Printing noises grow more menacing before sudden stop and blackout.

SCENE THIRTEEN

Penelope. Molly's bed,   **2 a.m. (17th June)**

Blackout broken by white spot on MOLLY.

MOLLY: I suppose it was him meeting Josie Breen and the funeral and thinking about me and Boylan set him off - well he can think what he likes now if thatll do him any good - I know him and Josie were spooning a bit when I came on the scene - I dont wonder because he was very handsome at that time - trying to look like lord Byron - it wasnt my fault she didnt darken the door much after we were married - I wonder what shes got like now after living with that dotty husband of hers - Denis Breen - the last time I saw her what was it she told me - O yes - that sometimes he used to go to bed with his muddy boots on when the maggot takes him - just imagine having to get into bed with a thing like that that might murder you any moment - Poldy anyway whatever he does always wipe his feet and blacks his own boots too - and now Breen going about in his slippers to look for £10000 for a postcard up up - O Sweetheart May wouldnt it simply bore you stiff to extinction - (*Pause, thinks*) I wonder who gave him that flower he said he bought

SCENE FOURTEEN

Laestrygonians. Dublin's streets, Burton's restaurant,   1 p.m.

BLOOM stands suspended until a passing PREACHER hands him a leaflet. BLOOM looks down staring at it.

BLOOM: (*Reads*)   Elijah is coming. Are you saved? Looks like those ads the quack doctor for the clap... (*Grips paper*) If Boylan... O.. No... No... *(Turns to see JOSIE BREEN approaching)* Josie... how do you do, Mrs Breen.

MRS BREEN: You're in black, Mr Bloom. You have no...

BLOOM: Dignan. An old friend of mine.

MRS BREEN: (*Melancholic, as if with hidden meaning*)   Sad to lose old friends.

BLOOM: (*To himself*)   Now that's quite enough about that. Same dress she had two years ago. Lines around her mouth. Only a year or two older than Molly. Just quietly: husband. (*To MRS BREEN*) And your lord and master?

MRS BREEN: Denis? Don't be talking. He's a caution to rattlesnakes. He has me heartscalded. Wait till I show you. (*Roots in handbag*) Do you know what he did last night? Woke me up. Dreams, he had, a nightmare. Said the ace of spades was walking up the stairs. (*Taking folded postcard from bag*) And now read that. He got it this morning.

BLOOM: (*Reading*)   What is it? U.P. Up.?

MRS BREEN: U.P.: up. Someone taking a rise out of him. (*Sighs, taking card back*) And now he's going to take an action for ten thousand pounds, he says.

BLOOM: (*Changing subject*)   Do you ever see anything of Mrs Purefoy?

MRS BREEN: She's in the lying-in hospital in Holles street. She's three days bad now. And a houseful of kids at home. It's a very stiff birth.

BLOOM: (*Tongue clacking in compassion*)   Three days! That's terrible for her.

MRS BREEN: *(Stares into distance)* There's Denis. I must go after him. Remember me to Molly, won't you?

BLOOM: *(Watching her go)* Poor Mrs Purefoy. *(Clacks tongue again)* Three days imagine groaning with a vinegared handkerchief round her forehead, her belly swollen out. *(Walks on, then stops)* I was happier then. Or was that I? Or am I now I? Twentyeight I was. Molly twentythree when we left Lombard street west something changed. She could never like it again after Rudy. Can't bring back time. Like holding water in your hand.

MARTHA: Are you not happy in your home, you poor naughty boy.

BLOOM: Wants to sew on buttons for me. I must answer. *(Pause)* Food. Try Burton's restaurant.

He turns as if opening a door to be confronted by CAST slobbering as they mime the most repulsive parodies of eating. ACTRESS D slovenly serves them with tray, their hands mauling her as she passes as if trying to tear at her flesh. Their voices merge.

ACTOR A: *(Roaring)* Roast beef and cabbage.

ACTOR B: More stew! More stew!

ACTOR C: Stout! Two stouts here!

ACTOR D: One corner and cabbage!

ALL TOGETHER: *(As BLOOM backs away in disgust)* Eat or be eaten! Kill! Kill! Kill! Kill!

BLOOM turns away, trying to prevent his stomach from heaving.

BLOOM: *(with difficulty)* Maybe not Burton's... a light snack instead...

CAST follow him, haunting his head as he crosses stage.

ACTORS: Poleaxe their skulls! Split them open! Trembling calves. Staggering bob. Bubble and squeak. Butchers' buckets wobble lights. Plup! Rawhead and bloody bones. Flayed glasseyed sheep. Lick it up, smoking hot, thick sugary blood!

BLOOM: *(Turning as they freeze)* Davy Byrne's pub. Take a glass of burgundy and... let me see... A cheese sandwich. Gorgonzola.

Lights fade, freezing him.

SCENE FIFTEEN

Wandering rocks, the streets of Dublin,   **3 p.m.**

Lights rise with an increase in music tempo. Everything is precisely choreographed, the stage alive with the bustle of a whole city. CAST are perpetually busy, forming shapes and clusters. FATHER COMMEE comes forward, patting pocket.

COMMEE: (*Pauses, thinking*)   Martin Cunningham's letter. The boy's name? Dignam, yes. Brother Swan in Artane is the person to see. Oblige, if possible.

ONELEGGED SAILOR, swinging himself onward on crutches, growls some notes and holds out a peaked cap towards COMMEE who blesses him and walks on. POSH LADY passes COMMEE, saluting respectfully. He doffs his silk hat to her as SCHOOLBOY almost collides with him. He steps back respectfully and COMMEE stoops to talk to him, producing an envelope for him to post. SCHOOLBOY runs off. COMMEE walks on, reading his office.

MOLLY'S voice is heard practicing. SAILOR jerks across the stage, swinging himself violently, growling.

SAILOR: For England, home and beauty.

He looks up in direction of MOLLY'S voice. SCHOOLBOY stares, open-mouthed, at his stump as SAILOR bays.

For England, home and beauty.

A coin clatters from a height onto the stage. SCHOOLBOY runs foward to give it to SAILOR.

BLAZES BOYLAN leans forward, handing a bottle of port and jar of perfume to SHOP GIRL.

BOYLAN: Put the port and perfume into the basket first, will you?

SHOP GIRL: Yes Mr Boylan, and the fruit on top?

BOYLAN: That'll do. Game ball. Can you send them at once by tram? Mrs Molly Bloom, 7 Eccles St. It's for an invalid.

SHOP GIRL: (*Leaning forward to write*)   Yes, Mr Boylan. I will, sir.

BOYLAN stares at the cut of her blouse as she leans forward to write, then he takes a red flower from a bunch on her dress.

BOYLAN: (*Flirtatiously*) This for me.

SHOP GIRL: (*Blushing, glancing sideways at him*) Yes, Mr Boylan.

BOYLAN sticks flower between his teeth and stares with even more intent into her blouse.

BOYLAN: (*Addressing her breasts*) May I say a word to your telephone, missy?

At back of stage SECRETARY types date carefully.

SECRETARY: 16th of June, nineteen hundred and four.

CAST create ringing phone noise. She lifts her hand to her ear.

Mr Boylan! Hello! That sports gentleman was looking for you. Lenehan, yes. He said he'd be in the Ormond Hotel at four.

LENEHAN crosses stage followed by M'COY.

M'COY: Lenehan. Where are you off to?

LENEHAN: Ah, M'Coy. I've to see Boylan over in the Ormond hotel at four. (*Turns*) Here, I want to pop in to see *Sceptre*'s starting price. What's the time by your gold watch and chain?

M'COY: (*Opening watch*) Just after three.

He turns but LENEHAN has gone. M'COY sees BLOOM'S back as BOOKSELLER holds pile of old books before him. LENEHAN returns.

LENEHAN: Even money. I knocked against Bantam Lyons in there going to back a bloody horse that hasn't an earthly. *Throwaway.* Given to him by (*Turns, sees BLOOM, voice scornful*) the very man.

M'COY: (*Disbelieving*) Bloom? Tip a horse? Wonder what he's buying over there? He's dead nuts for sales. I was with him one day and he bought a book for two bob. Stars and comets with long tails.

LENEHAN: (*Laughs*) I'll tell you a damn good one about comets' tails. There was a big spread out in Glencree reformatory.

M'COY: (*Trying to get in*) I know, Lenehan. My missus sang there once.

LENEHAN: Did she? (*Wheezy laugh*) But wait till I tell you, M'Coy. Yours truly was chief bottlewasher. Bloom and his wife were there. Lashings of stuff we put up: port wine and sherry.

M'COY: I know. The year the missus was there...

LENEHAN: But wait till I tell you. Coming home it was a gorgeous winter's night on the Featherbed Mountain. Bloom and Chris Callinan on one side of the car and I with his wife on the other, singing duets. She was well primed. Every jolt the bloody car gave I had her bumping against me. She has a fine pair. (*Forms shapes with his hands*) She's a gamey mare and no mistake. Bloom was pointing out the stars and comets, but, by God I was lost, so the speak, in the milky way. (*Gasps with soft laughter*) I'm weak, M'Coy.

LENEHAN sees M'COY'S grave disapproval. He walks on, trying to draw back, speaking in a serious tone.

He's a cultured allroundman, Bloom... not one of your common or garden... there's a touch of the artist about old Bloom.

As they walk away BLOOM hands book back to bookseller.

BOOKSELLER: (*Handing him more titles*) Them are two good books. *Fair Tyrants* by James Lovebirch.

BLOOM: The other. More in her line.

He flicks it open, suddenly engrossed in the prose.

ACTRESS A: (*Reciting*) Her mouth glued on his in a luscious voluptuous kiss while his hands felt for the opulent curves inside her deshabille.

BOOKSELLER, overcome with coughing, spits onto stage, wiping the sole of his boot across it.

BLOOM: (*Handing him the book*) I'll take this one.

BOOKSELLER: (*Tapping the cover*) Sweets of Sin. That's a good one.

BLOOM walks on, the bookseller is left motionless. DILLY DEDALUS waits nearby, miserable in tattered dress, with slumped shoulders. UNIFORMED BOY passes, ringing handbell.

BOY: Dillon's auctionrooms! Auction starting now inside!

DILLY looks up as SIMON DEDALUS approaches.

DEDALUS: (*Halts*) Stand up straight, daughter, for the love of the Lord Jesus. Do you know what you look like?

He parodies her stance. UNIFORMED BOY rings bell and exits.

DILLY: All the people are looking at you, father. Did you get any money?

DEDALUS: There is no-one in Dublin would lend Simon Dedalus fourpence.

DILLY: (*Looking into his eyes*) I know you got some. Were you in the Scotch house pub now?

DEDALUS: (*Smiling*) I was not then. (*Produces coin*) Here's a shilling, Dilly. See if you can do anything with that.

DILLY: Give me more than that.

DEDALUS: (*Threateningly*) You're like the rest of them, are you? An insolent pack of little bitches since your poor mother died. But wait awhile. I'm going to get rid of you.

He goes to brush past her, but DILLY catches up.

DILLY: You got more than that, father.

DEDALUS: I'll leave you all where Jesus left the jews. Look, that's all I have. (*Produces coins nervously*) I got two shillings from Jack Power and spent twopence for a shave for the funeral.

DILLY: (*Desperate*) Can't you look for some money somewhere?

DEDALUS: (*Handing her coins*) Here's twopence. Get a glass of milk or a bun or a something. (*Pockets rest and begins to walk on*) I'll be home shortly.

STEPHEN has crossed to take a book from BOOKSELLER'S pile.

BOOKSELLER: Twopence each. Four for sixpence.

STEPHEN: (*Reading titles*) The Irish Beekeeper. Pocket Guide to Killarney.

DILLY approaches him, holding a coverless book to her breast.

DILLY: What are you doing here, Stephen?

STEPHEN: (*Turning, surprised*) What have you there, Dilly?

DILLY: (*Showing him with nervous laugh*) I bought it from the other cart for a penny. Is it any good?

STEPHEN turns book over, flushed with sudden pity for her.

STEPHEN: Chardenal's French Primer. What did you buy that for? To learn French?

DILLY nods, reddening. He hands it back to her.

It's all right. Mind Maggy doesn't pawn it on you. I suppose all my schoolprizes are gone. Wondered would I find some here.

DILLY: Some of the books. We had to.

YOUNG DIGNAN (In mourning clothes) walks to centrestage. Light closes in on him as STEPHEN speaks.

STEPHEN: (*Softly, to himself*) She is drowning. My sister. All against us. She will drown me with her. Lank coils of seaweed hair around her, my heart, my soul. We.

YOUNG DIGNAM is left highlighted, everyone else in frozen silhouette. He stands as if staring into shop window.

BOY: That's me in the window in mourning. Too blooming dull sitting in the parlour and the blind down and they all at their sniffles. Uncle Barney said he'd get it into the paper tonight and everyone will read my name printed and pa's. The scrunch when they were screwing the screws into the coffin; and the bumps when they were bringing it downstairs. Never see him again. Pa is dead. He told me to be a good son to ma. I couldn't hear the other things he said but I saw his tongue and his teeth trying to say it better. That was Mr Dignam, my father.

Fade to blackout.

SCENE SIXTEEN

Penelope. Molly's bedroom,   **2 a.m. (17th June)**

Blackout is broken by white spot on MOLLY.

MOLLY: I hope hell come on Monday as he said - the messenger boy today - I thought it was a putoff first - him sending the port and peaches - and I was just beginning to yawn with nerves - thinking he was trying to make a fool of me when I knew his tattarrattat at the door - he must have been a bit late because it was 1/4 after 3 when I threw the penny to that lame sailor - then this day week were to go to Belfast - just as well he has to go to Ennis - his fathers anniversary - suppose our rooms at the hotel were beside each other and any fooling went on - I couldn't tell him to stop - its all very well a husband but you cant fool a lover - after me telling him we never did anything - no its better hes going where he is - I wonder will he take a first class - he might want to do it in the train by tipping the guard - suppose I never came back what would they say - eloped with him - that gets you on the stage...

Spot dies on MOLLY.

SCENE SEVENTEEN

Sirens. The Ormond Hotel,   **4 p.m.**

Penelope. Molly's bedroom,   **2 a.m.** **(17th June)**

Soft light picks up BLOOM alone centre stage. The backing track is that of an orchestra tuning up. CAST stand at back of stage, voices merging with disjointed, stop-and-start music.

ACTOR B: Horn. Hawthown.

ACTOR C: Martha! Come!

ACTRESS A: Listen!

ACTRESSES nip a peak of skirt above their knees to display a glimpse of flesh tauntingly, then lift garters to let them smack loudly against their thighs. BLOOM jerks his head, as if half-waking from sleep.

ACTORS: (*Sighing gleefully*)   La cloche!

ACTRESS B: Clapclop. Clipclap. Clappyclap.

Their hands clap briefly in unison. BLOOM starts, uncertainly.

ACTORS: Fro. To, fro. A baton cool protruding.

ACTRESSES: By bronze, by gold, in oceangreen of shadow. Bloom. Old Bloom.

ACTOR A: (*Steps forward, commanding voice*)   Sirens. Begin.

MISS KENNEDY crosses briefly to BLOOM, miming handing him a plate, then joins MISS DOUCE who has moved forward where a huge bar mirror and rack of bottles is lowered behind them. MISS DOUCE unblouses her neck. Backtrack is dominated by slow ticking.

MISS DOUCE: Am I awfully sunburnt, Miss Kennedy? I asked that old fogey in Boyd's for something for my skin.

MISS KENNEDY: (*Grimacing comically, plugging her ears*)   O, Miss Douce, don't remind me of him for mercy'sake!

MISS DOUCE: (*Grunting in snuffy fogey tone*)   For your what? says he.

Both shriek with helpless laughter.

MISS KENNEDY: Imagine being married to a man like that!

MISS DOUCE: (*Trying to control herself*)   Married to the greasy nose! O, saints above! I feel all wet!

MISS KENNEDY: (*Mock horror*) O,   Miss   Douce!   (*Looks around, whisper*) In the public bar of the Ormond hotel! You horrid thing!

SIMON DEDALUS approaches and they immediately control laughter and are charming to him.

MISS DOUCE: (*Letting him take her hand a moment*)   And what did the doctor order today, Mr Dedalus?

DEDALUS: Well now, I think I'll trouble you for some fresh water and a half glass of whisky.

LENEHAN enters, ignored by girls. MISS KENNEDY picks up book.

LENEHAN: Was Mr Boylan looking for me?

MISS DOUCE: (*Indifferently*) Miss   Kennedy?   Mr   Boylan looking for Mr Lenehan?

MISS KENNEDY: (*Not looking up*)   No. He was not.

LENEHAN: (*Touching the book which covers her face*)   Peep! Did she fall or was she pushed.

MISS KENNEDY: (*Slightingly, closing book*)   Ask no questions and you'll hear no lies, Mr Lenehan.

BLOOM: (*Looks down listlessly as if at plate*)   In   liver   gravy Bloom mashed mashed potato. Clean here at least. Best value in Dub.

BOYLAN enters, making a great noise with his smart tan shoes.

LENEHAN: (*Turning*)   See, Boylan, the conquering hero comes.

BOYLAN touches rim of straw hat to MISS KENNEDY who smiles sweetly at him.

BOYLAN: What's your cry, Lenehan? Glass of bitter? (*To MISS DOUCE*) Glass of bitter, please, and a sloegin for me. Gold Cup wire in yet?

LENEHAN: No yet.

LENEHAN, MISS KENNEDY and MISS DOUCE: At four!

MISS DOUCE stretches forward, breasts thrust deliberately in BOYLAN'S face. LENEHAN gasps, but BOYLAN remains cool. BLOOM rises and is halted by sight of BOYLAN in bar mirror. There is a sense of BLOOM watching, unnoticed by everyone. MISS DOUCE grasps bottle from rack and brings it down in triumph, smiling at BOYLAN as she pours drinks.

BOYLAN: What time is it? Four.

BLOOM shifts gaze from BOYLAN to slowly take out his watch.

BLOOM: Has he forgotten? At four. Perhaps a trick. Not come: whet appetite. I couldn't do. Wait.

BOYLAN: (*Singing to Miss Douce*) ...to Flora's lips did hie... (*Speaks beseechingly*) Please, please. (*Sings again*) I could not leave thee...

MISS DOUCE: (*Coyly*) Afterwits.

LENEHAN: (*Eagerly*) No, now. O do, Miss Douce. There's no-one.

Miss DOUCE looks to make sure nobody can see, then bends, watched closely by LENEHAN and singing BOYLAN. She nips a peak of skirt above her knee to display a glimpse of flesh tauntingly, then lets her garter smack loudly against her thigh. Lenehan sighs gleefully.

La cloche!

They are frozen into silhouettes. White spot returns to MOLLY.

MOLLY: he could buy me a nice present in Belfast after what I gave - better leave this ring behind or they might bell it round the town in their papers or tell the police - but theyd think were married - O let them all go and smother themselves for the fat lot I care - he has plenty of money and hes not a marrying man so somebody better get it out of him - if I could find out whether he likes me - scrooching down on me like that with his big hipbone - hes heavy too with his hairy chest for this heat - always having to lie down - better for him put it into me from behind the way Mrs Mastiansky told me her husband made her - like the dogs do it - and stick out her tongue as far as ever she could - can you ever be up to men - lovely stuff in that blue suit he had on - hes certainly well off - I know by the cut of his clothes - but he was like a perfect devil for a few minutes after he came back with the stop press - tearing up the tickets and swearing blazes because he lost 20 quid he said over that outsider that won - and half he put on for me - on account of Lenehans tip - cursing him to the lowest pits - that sponger that was making free with me after the Glencree dinner - coming back over the featherbed mountain

The white spot dies. Main lights switch back, releasing CAST.

MISS DOUCE: (*Smiling at Boylan*)   You're the essence of vulgarity, Mr Boylan.

She fixes her skirt as BOYLAN turns, impatient now.

BOYLAN: (*Finishing drink*)   I'm off.

LENEHAN: (*Surprised*)   Wait a shake, Boylan. I wanted to tell you...

BOYLAN: (*Turning to leave*)   Come on to blazes.

Ticking on soundtrack is louder, like a bomb.

LENEHAN: (*Gulping drink*)   Got the horn or what? Wait, I'm coming.

They exit, passing BEN DOLLARD who enters. BLOOM stands alone, watching DEDALUS drink in mirror. BOYLAN seizes a horse whip and cracks it, striding towards wing, his movements conveying his passing through a city and also a sense of muscular sexuality.

BLOOM: (*Head sinking*)   He's off. Jingling. He's gone. Jingle. Hear.

CHORUS OF ACTRESSES: Jogjaunty jingled Blazes Boylan, mare's glossy rump atrot.

LENEHAN: (*Voice merging*)   Horn. Have you the? Horn. Have you the? Haw haw horn.

CHORUS: (*Faster and continuous*)   Jogjaunty jingled Blazes Boylan, mare's glossy rump atrot.

DOLLARD: (*Breaking focus*)   Hoho, Simon Dedalus. Give us a ditty. Go on, blast you.

DEDALUS: (*Turning*) God be with old times, (*Listless*) My dancing days are done

LENEHAN: Horn. Have you the? Horn. Have you the? Haw haw horn.

DEDALUS: (*Holds out hands, mock speech*) Ladies and gentlemen, I would endeavour to sing to you of a heart bowed down. (*Begins to sing Aria from Flotow's **Martha**).

> When first I saw that form endearing
>
> Sorrow from me seemed to depart
>
> Full of hope and all delighted
>
> But alas, 'twas idle dreaming...

We sense BLOOM'S isolation and loss. DEDALUS' voice drops.

BLOOM: First night when first I saw her at Mat Dillon's in Terenure. Yellow, black lace she wore. Musical chairs. We too the last. Fate. Round and round slow. Quick round. We two. All looked. Halt. Down she sat. All ousted looked. Lips laughing. Yellow knees.

DEDALUS: (*Voice briefly rising*)

> Each graceful look
>
> Charmed my eye...

BLOOM: Singing. I turned her music. Full voice of perfume of what perfume does your lilactrees. Bosom I saw, both full, throat warbling. First I saw. She thanked me. Why did she me? Fate. Spanishy eyes. At me, luring. Ah, alluring.

CHORUS: Jingle by monument of one-handled Nelson, jaunted rump atrot.

LENEHAN: Atrot, in heat, slower the mare went up by rotunda.

CHORUS: Too slow for Boylan, Blazes Boylan, joggled the mare.

CHORUS: Jingle into Dorset street, impatience Boylan.

ALL: This is the jingle that joggled and jingled by Dlugacz' pork shop trotted a gallantbuttocked mare

DEDALUS: (*Full throated*) Martha! Ah, Martha!

> Co-me, thou lost one!
>
> Co-me, thou lost one!
>
> Come to me!

BARMAIDS and DOLLARD clap but sound is empty, hands not making contact. DOLLARD closes in on DEDALUS in slow motion, clapping him on back.

CHORUS: (*Continuing*)   Jogjaunty jingled Blazes Boylan, mare's glossy rump atrot.

BLOOM looks down at palm, as if reading off it.

BLOOM: (*Problem focusing*)   Miss Martha Clifford, c/o P.O. Dolphin's Barn lane. Dear Mady. Got your lett and flow. Hell do I put. It is utterl imposs. Underline *imposs*. to write today. Accept my poor little pres enclos: p.o. two and six. Why do you call me naught? You naughty too. Bye for today. My patience are exhaust. To keep it up. (*He looks up*) Folly am I writing. Husbands don't. Because I'm away from. Suppose. Keep young. If she found out. Useless pain.

CHORUS: Jog jigged jogged stopped.

LENEHAN: Dandy tan shoes, of dandy Boylan socks sky blue clocks came light to earth.

MISS KENNEDY has crossed stage. She passes BLOOM who turns his palm over, as if hiding the letter.

MISS KENNEDY: Out here alone, Mr Bloom. Answering an ad?

BLOOM: Yes. Town traveller. Nothing doing, I expect.

MISS KENNEDY: (*Walks on, stops to look back sadly*)   Under the sandwich bell lay on a bier of bread one last lonely sardine of summer. Bloom alone.

BLOOM: Fate, seems to be what you call yashmak or I mean kismet. Fate. (*Looks after MISS KENNEDY*) Crooked skirt swinging, whack by. (*Turns palm back over*) How will you punish? Tell me I want to know.

BOYLAN: (*Cracks whip in triumph*)   One rapped on a door, one tapped with a knock, did he nock Paul de Cock with a loud proud knocker, with a carra carra carra cock cock cock.

There is a tremendous pounding of a door knocker as light freezes them and finds MOLLY.

MOLLY: (*Breathless, reliving*)   yes because he must have come 3 or 4 times with that tremendous big red brute of a thing he has - I thought the vein - or whatever the dickens they call it - was going to burst - after my hours dressing and perfuming - like some kind of crowbar standing all the time - he must have eaten oysters - he was in great singing voice - no I never in all my life felt anyone had one the size of that - to make you feel full up - he must have eaten a whole sheep after - whats the idea making us with a big hole in the middle - like a Stallion driving it up into you - because thats all they want out of you - with that determined vicious look in his eye - I was coming for about 5 minutes with my legs around him - O Lord I wanted to shout out all sorts of things - fuck and shit

She gasps, crying out in orgasm. Blackout.

SCENE EIGHTEEN

Cyclops. Barney Kieran's pub,   **5 p.m.**

NARRATOR stands centre stage. THE CITIZEN reads paper in corner of bar, wearing an eye patch and scowling, with ACTRESS A (as his dog GARRYOWEN) at his feet and BARMAN in background. BOB DORAN (face obscured by hat) slumps drunkenly nearby.

NARRATOR: I was just passing the time of day at Arbour Hill and be damned but a bloody sweep near drove his gear into my eye. I turned to let him have the weight of my tongue when who should I see only Joe Hynes off *The Freeman.*

JOE HYNES approaches, whistling.

Lo, Joe. Did you see that bloody chimneysweep?

HYNES: Soot's luck. Come round to Barney Kiernan's pub. I want to see the citizen.

Both cross towards CITIZEN and GARRYOWEN.

NARRATOR: (*To audience*)   Sure enough there was the citizen up in the corner having a great confab with himself and that bloody mangy mongrel, Garryowen, and he waiting for what the sky would drop in the way of drink.

CITIZEN: (*Looking up as GARRYOWEN growls*)   Stand   and deliver!

NARRATOR: (*To audience*)   With his load of papers, working for the national cause.

HYNES: That's all right, citizen. Friends here.

GARROWEN growls savagely.

NARRATOR: (*To audience*) Be a corporal work of mercy if someone would take the life of that bloody dog. I'm told he ate a good part of the breeches off a constabulary man in Santry that came round one time about a licence.

CITIZEN: Pass, friends.

GARRYOWEN ceases growling.

HYNES: (*To BARMAN*) Three pints. (*To CITIZEN*) And how's the old heart, citizen?

CITIZEN: Never better, *a chara*. (*To dog*) What Garry? Are we going to win?

He grabs GARRYOWEN'S neck playfully and nearly throttles her.

NARRATOR: (*To audience*) That's the citizen, for you. A broadshouldered, deepchested, freely freckled, deepvoiced, hairy-legged hero. Last in line of many Irish heroes of antiquity, Cuchulin, Red Hugh O'Donnell, Christopher Columbus, The last of the Mohicans, Ludwig Beethoven, Jack the Giantkiller, Balor of the Evil Eye and O'Donovan Rossa.

CITIZEN releases dog's neck and pats her head as she struggles to recover her breath. HYNES pays for drink.

CITIZEN: (*Reading paper in outrage*) Listen to the deaths in the *Irish Independent*. English bloody names, every one.

HYNES: Ah, well, thanks be to God they had the start on us. Drink that citizen.

CITIZEN: (*Laying into pint*) I will, Hynes.

HYNES: (*After long gulp*) I was blue mouldly for the want of that pint. Declare to God I could hear it hit the pit of my stomach with a click.

ALF BERGAN slinks in, doubled with laughter. He signals to NARRATOR and both mime staring out window.

NARRATOR: (*Laughing*) In his bloody slippers with the unfortunate wife, Josie, hotfoot after him like a poodle.

HYNES: Who's that?

BERGAN: Denis Breen. He's traipsing all over Dublin with a postcard someone sent with with U.P.: up (*Mimes pissing upwards,* *then doubles with laughter*) on it to take a libel action for ten thousand pounds.

DORAN: (*Raising head drunkenly for first time*)   Is that Alf Bergan? Who are you laughing at? Is that you, Bergan?

NARRATOR: (*To audience*)   Says Bob Doran waking in the corner and he on one of his periodical bends.

DORAN: (*Aggressively*)   Who are you laughing at?

NARRATOR: I saw there was going to be a bit of dust. So says I just to make talk, (*To BERGAN*) How's Willy Murray these days, Alf?

BERGAN: I saw him just now in Capel Street with Paddy Dignam. Only I was...

HYNES: (*Shocked*)   With who?

BERGAN: With Dignam. Why?

HYNES: Don't you know he's dead?

BERGAN: Sure I'm after seeing him not five minutes ago.

HYNES: You saw his ghost then.

DORAN: What about Dignam? Who's talking about...?

BERGAN: Dead! He is no more dead than you are.

HYNES: Maybe so. They took the liberty of burying him this morning anyhow.

CITIZEN: (*Twisting neck as if staring through window*)   There he is again. Bloom. He's on point duty there for the last ten minutes.

NARRATOR: (*Turning to look, then to audience*)   And, begob, I saw Bloom's physog do a peep in and then slidder off again.

BERGAN: Good Christ, I could have sworn it was him.

DORAN: Who said Christ is good? (*Shouts*) He's a bloody ruffian, I say, to take away poor little Willy... little Paddy Dignam.

GARRYOWEN growls menacingly at BLOOM who enters.

CITIZEN: Come in, come on, he won't eat you.

BLOOM: (*To BARMAN*)   Has Martin Cunningham been in?

HYNES: (*Great friendliness*)   Hello, Bloom. What are you having?

NARRATOR: (*To audience*)   So they started arguing the point. Bloom saying he couldn't and no offence and then he'd just take a cigar.

HYNES: (*To BARMAN*)   Give us one of your prime stinkers, Terry.

GARRYOWEN sniffs BLOOM menacingly.

NARRATOR: (*To audience*)   Then everyone starts talking about capital punishment and of course Bloom comes out with all the codology... (*Looks at BLOOM*) I'm told these Jewies does have a queer odour coming off them for dogs.

BERGAN: There's one thing hanging hasn't a deterrent effect on.

HYNES: What's that?

BERGAN: The poor bugger's tool that's being hanged. The head warder in Kilmainham told me when they cut down Joe Brady, the invincible, it was standing up in their faces like a poker.

BLOOM: (*Rationally*)   That can be explained by science. It's only a natural phenomenon, don't you see, because...

NARRATOR: (*To audience*)   Herr Professor Luitpold Blumenduft with his jawbreakers.

BLOOM: (*Ignored, his words becoming just a background babble*) ...the instantaneous fracture of the cervical vertebrae and consequent scission of the spinal cord would be calculated to inevitably produce a violent ganglionic stimulus of the nerve centre, as to instantaneously facilitate the flow of blood to the penis or male organ, resulting in the pheonomenon of a morbid philoprogenitive erection...

GARRYOWEN has left BLOOM. DORAN tries to grab her paw while BERGAN tries to prevent DORAN falling onto the dog.

NARRATOR: (*To audience*)   But of course the citizen is only waiting to start gassing out of him about the invincibles and all the fellows who were hanged, drawn and transported for the cause of a new Ireland.

DORAN: (*To BARMAN*)   Give us over that biscuit tin, few old biscuits for the doggy.

NARRATOR: (*To audience*)   And the citizen and Bloom having an argument about some point...

BARMAN hands DORAN a Jacob's biscuit tin which he drops down for DOG to push violently across stage, as CITIZEN raises pint and glares.

CITIZEN: The memory of the dead!

HYNES: Ay, ay.

BLOOM: You don't grasp my point. What I mean is...

CITIZEN: *Sinn Fein amhain!* The friends we love are by our side and the foes we hate before us.

DOG leaves tin to sniff NARRATOR who eyes her distastefully. CITIZEN switches gaze from BLOOM to sneer.

Afraid he'll bite you?

NARRATOR: No. But he might take my leg for a lamppost.

CITIZEN: Here Garry.

HYNES: (*To Citizen*)   Could you make a hole in another pint?

CITIZEN: I will, *a chara*, to show there's no ill feeling.

HYNES: (*To barman*)   Same again. And yourself, Bloom?

BLOOM: Thank you, no. As a matter of fact I just wanted to meet Martin Cunningham, don't you see, to sort out this insurance of poor Dignam's. Martin asked me to go to the house.

DORAN: (*Staggers over to shake BLOOM'S hand*)   Let me presume upon our acquaintance to request the favour of you telling Mrs Dignam that Bob Doran said there was never a truer, a finer than poor little Willy that's dead.

HYNES: (*Bringing down drinks*)   Here, citizen. Fortune. Good health.

CITIZEN: (*Taking huge swallow*)   *Slan leat.*

DORAN staggers offstage.

BERGAN: I hear Blazes Boylan's running a concert tour now up in the north.

BLOOM: That's quite true. A kind of summer tour, you see. Just a holiday.

HYNES: Mrs B. is the bright particular star, isn't she?

BLOOM: My wife. She's singing yes. He's an excellent man to organise.

BERGAN: (*Peering through window*)   That bloody lunatic Breen is out there again. (*Laughs*) God, I'd give anything to hear him before a judge and jury.

BLOOM: Still, on account of the poor woman, I mean his wife.

CITIZEN: Pity about her. Or any other woman marries a fellow that's neither fish nor flesh.

NARRATOR: (*To audience*) Begob, I saw there was trouble coming. Bloom letting on he heard nothing and talking away with Joe Hynes about fixing up some ad to do about keys, when in walks the sports boyo Lenehan with a face on him as long as a late breakfast.

LENEHAN enters.

CITIZEN: The Saxon robbers. We let them come in. A dishonoured wife, that's what's the cause of all our misfortunes. To hell with the bloody brutal Sassenachs and their *patois*.

NARRATOR: (*To audience*) And Bloom starts trying to tell him about their moderation and botheration and their civilisation.

CITIZEN: Their syphilisation, you mean. Any civilisation they have they stole from us. Tonguetied sons of bastard's ghosts.

CITIZEN drains his pint in fury.

NARRATOR: (*To Lenehan*) What's up with you?

LENEHAN: Gold Cup.

BARMAN: Who won, Mr Lenehan?

LENEHAN: *Throwaway* at twenty to one. A rank outsider. We're all in the cart. Boylan plunged two quid on my tip *Sceptre* for himself and a lady friend. *Throwaway*. Takes the biscuit.

HYNES: (*Cheerfully*) Keep your pecker up. She'd have won only for the other dog. Will you try another one, citizen?

CITIZEN: Yes sir, I will.

NARRATOR: Beholden to you, Joe. (*To audience*) The drink was flowing and the citizen arguing about law and history with Bloom sticking in the odd word.

BLOOM: Persecution. All the history of the world is full of it. Perpetuating national hatred among nations.

LENEHAN: But do you know what a nation means?

BLOOM: Yes. A nation is the same people living in the same place.

BERGAN: (*Laughing*) By God, then if that's so I'm a nation for I'm living in the same place for the last five years.

CITIZEN: What is your nation, if I may ask?

BLOOM: Ireland. I was born here. Ireland.

CITIZEN looks at BLOOM, then spits into corner and dries himself with his handkerchief.

HYNES: (*Bring down pints*)   Here you are citizen. Take that in your right hand and repeat after me.

NARRATOR: (*Reaching across for glass*)   Shove us over the drink. Which is which?

HYNES: (*Indicating*)   That's mine, as the devil said to the dead policeman.

BLOOM: And I belong to a race too that is hated and persecuted. This very moment. This very instant. (*Waving cigar*) Robbed. Plundered. Insulted. Persecuted.

CITIZEN: Are you talking about the new Jersualem?

BLOOM: I'm talking about injustice.

BERGAN: Right. Stand up to it with force like men.

BLOOM: But it's no use. Force, hatred, history, all that. That's not life for men and women, insult and hatred. And everybody knows that it's the very opposite of that that is really life.

BERGAN: What?

BLOOM: Love. I mean the opposite of hatred. (*Turns*) I must go now. Just around the corner to see if Martin is there. If he comes just say I'll be back in a second.

NARRATOR: Who's hindering you?

BLOOM exits.

BERGAN: Well, that's what we're told? Love your neighbours.

CITIZEN: That chap? Beggar my neighbour is his motto.

NARRATOR: (*Supping pint*)   Well, Joe. Your very good health and song. More power, citizen.

All drink. BERGAN drains glass and exits.

LENEHAN: I know where he's gone.

NARRATOR: Who?

LENEHAN: Bloom. The courthouse is a blind. He had a few bob on *Throwaway* and he's gone to gather in the shekels.

CITIZEN: Is it that whiteyed kaffir, that never backed a horse in anger.

LENEHAN: I met Bantam Lyons going to back that horse only I put him off it and he told me Bloom gave him the tip when he asked to see Bloom's paper this morning. Bet you what you like he has a hundred shillings to five on. He's the only man in Dublin has it. A dark horse.

HYNES: He's a bloody dark horse himself.

NARRATOR: (*To audience*) Soon they were at it dingdong. God save Ireland from the likes of that bloody mouseabout, Mr Bloom and his old fellow before him perpetrating frauds, old Methusalem Bloom, the robbing bagman, that poisoned himself, when who comes in only Martin Cunningham.

CUNNINGHAM enters.

CUNNINGHAM: Where's Bloom?

LENEHAN: (*Bitterly*) Where is he, Cunningham? Defrauding widows and orphans.

NARRATOR: Who the hell is he anyhow? Isn't he a cousin of Bloom the dentist?

CUNNINGHAM: Not at all. He's a perverted jew from a place in Hungary and it was he drew up all the plans according to the Hungarian system. We know that in Dublin Castle. His real name was Virag. The father's name that poisoned himself. He changed it by deed poll, the father did.

CITIZEN: That's the new Messiah for Ireland.

CUNNINGHAM: Well they're still waiting for their redeemer. For that matter so are we.

NARRATOR: Yes, and every male that's born they think it may be their Messiah. And every jew is in a tall state of excitement, I believe, till he knows if he's a father or a mother.

HYNES: O, by God, you should have seen Bloom before that son of his that died was born. I met him buying a tin of Neave's food six weeks before the wife was delivered.

CITIZEN: (*Scornfully*) Do you call that a man?

LENEHAN: Well, there were two children born anyhow.

CITIZEN: And who does he suspect?

NARRATOR: Gob, there's many a true word spoken in jest.

CUNNINGHAM: Charity to the neighbour. But where is he? We can't wait.

CITIZEN: A wolf in sheep's clothing. That's what he is. Virag from Hungary!

BLOOM returns and sees CUNNINGHAM.

BLOOM: I was just round at the courthouse looking for you. I hope I'm not...

CITIZEN: Don't tell anyone.

BLOOM: (*Puzzled*) Beg your pardon?

CUNNINGHAM: (*Trying to take his arm*) Come on Bloom, come along now.

CITIZEN: (*Roaring*) Don't tell anyone. It's a secret.

GARRYOWEN wakes at his feet and begins to growl at BLOOM.

CUNNINGHAM: (*Ushering BLOOM away*) Bye bye all. (*To BLOOM*) Out, up onto the cart.

CITIZEN: (*Rising to follow BLOOM with a roar*) Courthouse my eye and your pockets hanging down with gold and silver. Stand us a drink itself. There's a jew for you! Cute as a shithouse rat. Hundred to five. (*HYNES tries to pull him back*) Jew! Jew! Three cheers for Israel!

LENEHAN joins HYNES in trying to hold the CITIZEN while CUNNINGHAM pulls BLOOM up onto platform where JARVEY with whip waits.

BLOOM: (*Pulling away from CUNNIGHAM*) Mendelssohn was a jew and Karl Marx and Spinoza. And the Saviour was a jew and his father was a jew. Your God.

CUNNINGHAM: He had no father. That will do now. (*Pushes JARVEY urgently*) Drive ahead, jarvey.

BLOOM: Well, his uncle was a jew. Your God was a jew. Christ was a jew like me.

CITIZEN: (*Breaking from grip to dart backwards*) By Jesus, I'll brain that bloody jewman for using the holy name. By Jesus, I'll crucify him so I will. (*To NARRATOR*) Give us that biscuitbox here.

NARRATOR, who has been finishing his own and several other pints, ignores him. CITIZEN grabs the biscuit box with HYNES and LENEHAN again trying to hold him. He manages to throw it in BLOOM'S direction, with all roaring.

CITIZEN: Did I kill him or what? (*To dog*) After him, Garry!

As CUNNINGHAM pushes JARVEY who flicks whip, the chasing party stop suddenly and sink to their knees, gazing in wonder at BLOOM who is flooded by a shaft of light. His head is thrown back, hands outstretched in the pose of a charioteer. NARRATOR lowers pint to stare.

NARRATOR: And, lo, there came about them a great brightness and they beheld the chariot wherein He stood ascend to heaven. And there came a voice out of heaven, calling: Elijah! Elijah! And they beheld Him, ben Bloom Elijah, amid clouds of angels ascend to glory at an angle of fortyfive degrees over Donohoe's in Little Green Street, like a shot off a shovel.

He drowns pint. Blackout.

End of Act One.

ACT TWO

SCENE ONE

Nausikaa. Sandymount Strand,   **8 p.m.**

Lights come up. GERTY MacDOWELL, CISSY CAFFREY and EDY BOARDMAN are seated at back right of stage. BLOOM leans against shape (stylised shape of hull of boat) at front of stage. GERTY sits in pensive silence, slightly apart from others, glancing towards BLOOM. Edy rocks an old perambulator. The bedstead has become a pulpit where PRIEST opens up a heavy tone. Others of the cast kneel before him, as if men in church. TOMMY and JACKIE CAFFREY scamper about, as four year old boys, with sailor caps, playing with buckets and spades. Light on PRIEST and CONGREGATION is muffled and stainglassed, while on BLOOM/GERTY it suggests evening light.

PRIEST: (*Reciting*) The summer evening has begun to fold the world in its mysterious embrace.

CONGREGATION: (*Reciting back*) The sun's last glow lingers lovingly on Sandymount shore.

PRIEST: And on this quiet church whence there streams forth from the men's temperance retreat...

CONGREGATION: The voice of prayer to her who is a radiant beacon to the stormtossed heart of man...

PRIEST AND CONGREGATION: Mary, star of the sea.

EDY: (*Peering into pram*) Now, baby, say it big. I want a drink of water.

JACKY: (*Turning head as he pushes TOMMY*) A jink a jink a jawbo.

CISSY: (*Scolding*) Nasty, bold Jacky to throw poor Tommy in the sand. Wait till I catch you.

TOMMY approaches CISSY tearfully and she puts an arm around him.

EDY: (*To TOMMY*) Tell us, Tommy Caffrey, who is your sweetheart. Is it Cissy? Your sister?

TOMMY: (*Shy, tearful, shifting legs*)   Nao.

CISSY: (*Glance at EDY*)   Is Edy Boardman your sweetheart?

TOMMY: (*Jigging slightly*)   Nao.

EDY: (*Arch glance at GERTY*) I know who is Tommy's sweetheart. Gerty MacDowell is.

TOMMY: (*Almost in pain*)   Nao.

GERTY decides against retorting, and resumes staring at BLOOM.

CISSY: (*Whisper to EDY*)   O, take him behind the pushcart where the gentleman can't see and mind he doesn't wet his new tan shoes.

EDY and TOMMY exit.

PRIEST: Her figure slight and graceful...

CONGREGATION: In its ivorylike purity...

PRIEST: And her chief care...

CONGREGATION: And who that knows the fluttering hopes of seventeen can blame her...

PRIEST: Are her undies...

CONGREGATION: Her four dinky pairs with pretty stitchery...

PRIEST: Rosepink, pale blue, mauve and peagreen...

CONGREGATION: And she is wearing the blue for luck...

PRIEST: Hoping against hope. Her strained look that is infinitely sad and wistful. Gerty McDowell yearning in vain for weddingbells to ring for her as Mrs Reggy Wylie.

GERTY: (*Entranced, to herself*)   Mrs... Reggy... Wylie...

EDY: (*Offstage. To TOMMY*)   Are you done?

EDY emerges with TOMMY, buttoning his flies before he runs to push JACKY who plays with a ball.

GERTY: It would be like heaven. For riches for poor, in sickness in health. A cosy little homely house with chintz covers for the chairs and over the mantlepiece that photograph of grandpapa's lovely dog that can almost talk it's so human... Garryowen. (*Sighs*) This waiting, always waiting to be asked.

EDY: (*Coarse call, breaking spell*) Tommy, stop that pushing or I'll give you something, where I won't say.

CISSY: (*Laughing merrily*) On the beetoteetom.

GERTY: (*Shocked, with sharp look to CISSY and then BLOOM*) Cissy!

CISSY: (*Looks at BLOOM with pert toss of head*) Let the man hear! Give it to him too on the same place as quick.

GERTY looks down embarrassed as priest and congregation begin a mumbled hymn. GERTY looks sadly towards the singing as TOMMY kicks a ball towards BLOOM.

CISSY: (*Calling*) Could you throw it back please, Sir.

BLOOM picks the ball up, aims and rolls it towards GERTY'S feet. Both twins clamour for it.

Kick it away Gerty, let them fight over it.

GERTY hesitates, kicks awkwardly and misses as girls laugh. She glances at BLOOM, embarrassed, then tries again. The twins run after it, followed by CISSY and EDY.

PRIEST: Virgin most powerful, virgin most merciful...

CONGREGATION: Pray for us...

PRIEST: Conceived without stain of original sin...

CONGREGATION: Pray for us...

PRIEST: Spiritual vessel, honourable vessel...

CONGREGATION: Pray for us...

PRIEST: Pray for the careworn hearts here, the toilers for their daily bread, the many who have erred and wandered, eyes wet with contrition...

GERTY: (*Glancing after girls, then at BLOOM*) For goodness sake, take your squalling baby and brats of twins home out of that and not be getting on my nerves.

PRIEST: (*Closing book as if about to preach sermon and turning to look at GERTY*) Yes. Because it was her the gentleman was looking at and while she gazed her heart went *pitapat, pitapat*. His eyes burned into her as though they would read her very soul.

GERTY: (*Begins to swing foot thoughtfully*) In deep mourning, he is and the story of a haunting sorrow written on his face. Like nobody else. Perhaps he can see the buckles of my shoes.

CONGREGATION: (*Chant*) Refuge of sinners. Comfortress of the afflicted.

PRIEST: Her girlheart went out to him, her dreamhusband. If he had suffered or even if he had been himself a sinner she cared not.

GERTY: (*Stares dreamily at BLOOM*) Even if he's a protestant or a methodist I can convert him easily if he truly loves me.

GERTY has not noticed EDY and CISSY creeping up behind her.

EDY: (*Surprising GERTY*) A penny for your thoughts.

GERTY: (*Drawn back into the present*) I was just wondering was it late.

CISSY: I'll ask Uncle Peter what's the time by his conundrum.

CISSY goes over to BLOOM who takes out his watch, looks at it, gives it a shake, then begins to wind it.

PRIEST: And she could see him getting nervous. Passionate nature though he had, he had enormous control. One minute fascinated by loveliness, and the next moment becoming a quiet gentleman, though Gerty could hear the suspicion of a quiver in his measured tones.

CISSY: (*Putting tongue out as she returns*) Uncle thinks it's after eight, but his waterworks is out of order.

EDY and CISSY begin to tidy themselves and the twins, while GERTY remains where she is, starting to swing her leg more explicitly in and out in time. The stage has been darkening (as in a sunset), except for the space around her.

PRIEST: It was getting darker and he was looking all the time and then he put the watch back and put his hands in his pockets. A kind of sensation rushed all over her and she knew by the feel of her scalp that the thing must be coming on. His eyes worshipped at her shrine.

GERTY: (*Breathless*) That admiration is for me! Oh!

EDY: (*Calling*) Come on, Gerty.

There are sudden coloured flashes across the backdrop. The girls and twins look towards them.

CISSY: (*Excitedly*)   It's fireworks. Come on, Gerty. It's the bazaar fireworks.

They run to edge of stage. BLOOM and GERTY continue their activities more openly now. GERTY leans back, catching her knee with her hand. CONGREGATION begin to pant and moan softly.

PRIEST: And they all ran to see it over the church, helterskelter. But if they could run like rossies she could sit. Whitehot passion was in his face, and it made her his. At last they were alone. His hands were working and a tremor went over her. She leaned back far to look up at the fireworks and there was no-one to see only him and she seemed to hear the panting of his heart and hoarse breathing.

JACKY: (*Pointing and shouting*)   Look! Another!

PRIEST: And they all shouted to look, look, and she leaned back ever so far and something queer was flying about through the air, a soft thing to and fro, dark. And she saw a long Roman candle over the trees, up, up, and they were breathless with excitement as it went higher and higher and she had to lean back more and more, high, high, almost out of sight, and he could see her other things too and then it went so high she was trembling in every limb from he had a full view, no one ever, and she wasn't ashamed and he wasn't either. And then a rocket sprang and burst and it was like a sigh of O! (*BLOOM crumbles forward, gasping, lifting his hand from pocket*) and everyone cried O! in raptures and it gushed out a stream of rain gold hair threads and ah! they were all greeny dewy stars falling with golden, O so lovely! O so sweet, soft! (*GERTY slowly straightens herself*) Then all melted away, all was silent. She glanced at him, shy reproach. (*Colder voice*) Leopold Bloom, for it is he, stands silent, with bowed head, before those young guileless eyes. At it again!

CISSY: (*Whistling rudely*)   Gerty! Come on. We can see from further up.

GERTY stands reluctantly, with a last half glance at BLOOM. She draws herself to her full height, but as she walks a limp spoils her image of grace and beauty.

PRIEST: Slowly, without looking back she went back up the uneven strand to Cissy, to Edy, to Jacky and Tommy Caffrey, to little baby Boardman. It was darker now and there were stones and slippery seaweed. She walked with a certain quiet dignity but with care and slowly because Gerty MacDowell was...

BLOOM: (*In bitter disappointment*)   Tight boots? No. She's lame! O!

GERTY exits after girls. BLOOM carefully pulls out his shirt.

That little limping devil. Wet shirt. Begin to feel cold and clammy. Still you have to get rid of it somewhere. They don't care. Go home to nicey bread and milky and night prayers with the kiddies. (*Adjusting clothes*) Tired I feel now. Will I get up? O wait. Drained the manhood out of me. (*Looks beyond the audience*) All quiet over there on Howth Head now. Where we. I am a fool perhaps. Boylan gets the plums and I the plumstones. My youth. Never again. Gibraltar. Evenings like this looking out over the sea, she told me, but clear, no clouds. (*Picks up piece of stick*) Said she always thought she'd marry a lord or a gentleman with a private yacht. Why me?

MOLLY: (*Distant whisper V/O*)   Because you were so foreign from the others.

BLOOM: (*Writing as if to GERTY with stick in sand*)   I...   AM... A...

MOLLY: (*Mocking whisper V/O*)   Stick in the mud, Poldy.

BLOOM drops stick and wipes the letters with his boot. He leans back, closes his eyes, drifts towards sleep.

BLOOM: (*Sleepily*)   Those lovely seaside girls, all... (*yawns*) just for a few...

He yawns again and is still. GERTY returns to edge of stage to glance towards him. On the backing track a cuckoo clock strikes the hour, cuckoo noise fading away with blackout.

SCENE TWO

Penelope. Molly's bed,   **2 a.m. (17th June)**

Blackout broken by a white spot on MOLLY.

MOLLY: I felt lovely and tired myself afterwards and fell asleep the moment I popped into bed - till that thunder woke me - as if the world was coming to an end - God be merciful - I thought the heavens were coming down to punish when I blessed myself and said a Hail

Mary - like those awful thunderbolts in Gibraltar - and they tell you theres no God - what could you do nothing only make an act of contrition - hed scoff because he never goes to church mass or meeting - he says you have no soul inside only grey matter - because he doesn't know what it is to have one

Spotlight fades.

SCENE THREE

Oxen of the Sun. Holles street Hospital,   **10 p.m.**

ACTOR B crosses empty stage, like a traveller from the Middle Ages. He glances about to make sure he is alone, then speaks in hushed, confiding tones. At different stages his posture and delivery will suggest changing personas.

ACTOR B: Among the celts the art of medicine was highly honoured. Not to speak of hostels, leperyards, sweating chambers. A plan was by them adopted whereby whatever care the patient in that allhardest of woman hour chiefly required was given her in houses of maternity by midwives attended.

But look! Some wayfaring man was stood by such a housedoor at night's oncoming. In the street of Holles where teeming mothers are wont to lie. And that man of Israel's folk, this Bloom, then asked how it fared with the woman, Purefoy. The nursing woman answered him that the woman Purefoy was in throes now full three days, that she had seen none so hard as was that woman's birth.

And whiles they spake a door was opened and there nighed them a mickle noise as of many young learning knights at meat. And they would not hear say nay but that the traveller Leopold make merry with them. And so he went in for to rest being sore of limb and took a draught for to pleasure the learning knights for he drank no manner of mead and anon he voided the most part in his neighbour's glass.

Now let us speak of that drunken fellowship. There were right witty scholars of medicine; one Lenehan, older than the others, a sport gentleman and what belonged of women, horseflesh or scandal he had it pat; and, at the head of the board, young Stephen, son of Dedalus, and he of a wild manner when he was drunken and that he was now.

But sir Leopold had pity of the shrieking of women in their labour above and was minded of his good lady Marion that had borne him an only manchild which on his eleventh day had died, and now sir Leopold that had no manchild for an heir looked upon his friend Dedalus' son and grieved for that he lived riotously with those wastrels and murdered his goods with whores.

Hereupon a black crack of thunder in the street bawled back. And one knight bade Stephen have a care as the god self was angered by his paganry. And young Stephen was of a sudden quite plucked down and his heart shook. Then did some mock while Master Bloom spoke to him calming words, advertising how all was of the order of a natural phenomenon.

ACTOR'S voice and manner changes here.

And as the students drank, our worthy acquaintance, Mr Malachi Mulligan, appeared with a young gentleman, Alec Bannon, who had late arrived from Mullingar. Mr Mulligan now perceiving the stranger, Bloom, made him a bow and said, Pray, sir, was you in need of any professional assistance? The stranger replied that he was come about a lady, Purefoy, to know if her happiness had yet taken place. Whereupon Mr Mulligan, in a gale of laughter, smote himself bravely, exclaiming with an admirable mimic of Mother Grogan: There's a belly that never bore a bastard. This threw the room into the most violent agitations of delight.

Amid the general hilarity a nurse entered, and having spoken to young Mister Dixon, retired. The departure of that woman endured with every quality of modesty was the signal for an outbreak of ribaldy. Strike me silly, a monstrous bit of cowsflesh! The young surgeon, however rose to say he was needed. Merciful providence had been pleased to put a period to the suffering of the lady, Purefoy, and she had given birth to a bouncing boy.

But to revert to Mr Bloom, no longer is Leopold, as he sits ruminating, that staid agent of publicity. Now he sees himself paternal and these about him might be his sons. Who can say? The wise father knows his own child. No, Leopold. No son of thy loins is by thee.

ACTOR'S voice drops a moment in sorrow, then his arms fling out, changing again.

"Burke's pub!" Outflings my lord Stephen, giving the cry, and a tag and bobtail of all them after with punctual Bloom at heels. They are out tumultuously, all bravely legging it. Burke's their ulterior goal. Bloom stays to send a kind word to happy mother and nurseling up there. The air without is impregnated with raindew moisture, glistering on Dublin stone. Burke's! Thence they advanced. Slattery's mounted foot where's that bleeding awfur? Yours? Mead of our father. Hurroo! Lang may your lum reek and your kailpot boil! My tipple. Here's to us! Steve boy, you're going it some. Landlord, get ye gone. Forward woozy wobblers! Night, Night. The Leith police dismisseth us. Who will go with Stephen? Lynch! The whores of Nighttown this way. Westland Row Station. Change here for Bawdyhouse. We two will seek the kips where shady Mary is.

ACTOR waves arms, as though directing them, then turns into an American preacher from the Deep South.

Come on, you dog-gone, bullnecked, weaseleyed, four-flushers! Alexander J. Christ Dowie, that's yanked to glory most half this planet from 'Frisco Beach to Vladivostok. Shout salvation in king Jesus. He's got a coughmixture with a punch in it for you, my friend, in his backpocket. Just you try it on.

Stage dissolves into darkness.

SCENE FOUR

Circe. Nighttown and the house of Bella Cohen,   **11.15 p.m.**

Lights rise, with distance tinkle of pianola, on intense street bustle. Two sofas and a pianola are laid out to top left of stage where a gas chandelier is lowered with CISSY CAFFREY swinging out of it. She jumps down and runs about with the others, then jumps onto what is lit as a run-down street, mumbling rubbish to herself. The lighting is shifty, figures crossing in and out of shadows. There is disjointed raucous laughter, whistles. DEAFDUMB IDIOT stomps about, dribbling, limbs flailing. URCHIN shoves him mercilessly on.

URCHIN: Kithogue! Salute.

IDIOT: (*Lifting palsied left arm and gurgling*)   Grhahute!

CISSY: (*Singing shrilly on swing*)

      I gave it to Molly

      Because she was jolly,

      The leg of the duck

      The leg of the duck.

URCHIN releases IDIOT who stumbles offstage. PRIVATES CARR and COMPTON march unsteadily on, turn aboutface and burst from their mouths a volleyed fart. There is laughter from shadows.

ELDERLY BAWD: (*Retorting*) Signs on you, hairy arse! More power the Cavan girl!

SOLDIERS jeer and move on, almost bumping into STEPHEN (who flourishes ashplant and chants with drunken joy) and LYNCH, with a jockey cap low on brow.

PRIVATE CARR: (*After Stephen*) What ho, parson!

CISSY: (*Swinging higher*)
    She has it, she got it,
    Wherever she put it
    The leg of the duck.

LYNCH, glancing back at SOLDIERS, pushes STEPHEN on.

BAWD: (*Beckoning them with husky whisper*) Sst! Come here till I tell you. Maidenhead inside.

STEPHEN: Et omnes ad quos pervenit aqua ista.

BAWD: (*Spitting after them with venom*) Trinity medicals. All prick and no pence.

LYNCH: Where are we going?

STEPHEN: (*Thrusts ashplant at him, holds out hands expansively*) To *la belle dame sans merci*, Lynch. Georgina Johnson.

LYNCH thrusts his stick back at him as they exit. BLOOM enters, panting, cramming chocolate into a pocket.

BLOOM: Stitch in my side. Why did I run after young Dedalus? (*Deep breath*) I'll miss him. Better run. Quick.

CYCLIST (in goggles and hat) appears behind BLOOM, riding heavy delivery bicycle. BLOOM turns, almost colliding with him. CYCLIST swerves, ringing bell loudly.

CYCLIST: Hey, shitbreeches, mind your arse!

BLOOM steps back frightened and, as he turns, collides with URCHIN who runs full tilt into him. BLOOM staggers back, shocked as he runs off. CISSY jumps from swing to follow him.

BLOOM: *(Pats his clothes)* Old pickpockets' dodge. Collide. Then snatch your purse.

Street noises stop. Lighting switches, highlighting and distorting the raised bedstead, creating a surreal arena which looks down upon BLOOM and the real street. While this area is in use actions can still take place in real world, but nobody there (except BLOOM) has an awareness of it. BLOOM's father, RUDOLPH, stooped and in the long caftan, with smoking cap and horned spectacles, appears.

RUDOLPH: *(Sternly)* I told you not go with drunken goy ever. What you making down this place? Have you no soul? Are you not my dear son Leopold, grandson of Leopold, who left the house of his father and the god of his fathers Abraham and Jacob?

BLOOM: *(With precaution)* I suppose so, father. Mosenthal. All that's left of him.

RUDOLPH: *(Severely)* One night they bring you home drunk as dog after spend your good money. Mud head to foot. *(With contempt)* Nice spectacles for your poor mother!

ELLEN BLOOM, hair plaited in crispine net and holding slanted candlestick, appears beside Rudolph.

ELLEN BLOOM: *(Shrill alarm)* O blessed Redeemer, what have they done to my son? Sacred Heart of Mary, where were you at all?

BLOOM mumbles, eyes downcast, the shamed son. MOLLY suddenly pokes her head between BLOOM's parents, dressed in Turkish costume with a white yashmak covering her face and a coin gleaming on her forehead.

MOLLY *(Sharply)* Poldy!

BLOOM *(Ducking to ward off a blow)* Who? At your service. *(Looks up)* Molly!

MOLLY *(Sternly)* Mrs Marion from this out, my dear man. *(Satirically)* Has poor little hubby cold feet waiting so long?

BLOOM: *(In agitation)* No. Not the least little bit... Mrs. Marion... *(Stares, spellbound)* if you...

MOLLY: So you notice some change? *(Friendly mockery)* O Poldy, you are a poor old stick in the mud! *(Softly, retreating in disdain)* Go and see life. See the wide world, Poldy.

Lights switch. Back in real world BAWD seizes BLOOM'S sleeve.

BAWD: Ten shillings a maidenhead. Fresh thing was never touched. There's no-one in it only her old father that's dead drunk.

She points towards shadows where GIRL now stands, barefoot, in ragged white shift, finger in mouth as she sways furtively. ACTOR A clasps her roughly. She laughs as she is dragged away.

THE BAWD: (*Wolfeyes shining*) He's getting his pleasure. Ten shillings. Don't be all night before the polis in plain clothes sees us.

VOICE OF GERTY MacDOWELL: (*From bedstead*) Dirty married man!

BAWD (*Shouts*) Leave the gentleman alone! Better for your mother to take the strap to you at the bedpost, you hussy!

A pair of girl's boots and then legs appear through bedstead until GERTY'S blue undies are on display. GERTY stares at BLOOM as BAWD tugs at him and spits as he steps away into surreal light.

GERTY: When you saw all the secrets of my bottom drawer. Dirty married man!

BLOOM: You're dreaming. I never saw you before.

GERTY: (*Withdrawing her legs*) I loved you for doing that to me.

MRS BREEN appears, eyes roguishly as she smiles at him.

MRS BREEN: Mr Bloom! Down in the haunts of sin! Caught you nicely!

BLOOM: (*In alarm*) Don't give me away, Mrs Breen. Short cut home. Rescue of fallen women Magdalen asylum. I am the secretary...

MRS BREEN: Now don't tell a big fib! (*Slyly*) I know a certain Molly won't like that.

BLOOM: (*Glance around him*) She often said she'd like to visit. Slumming. The exotic, you see. (*Bolder*) Would you like me perhaps to embrace you just for a second?

MRS BREEN: (*Screams gaily*) O, you ruck!

BLOOM: (*Seizing her wrist*) For old sake' sake. You know I had a soft corner for you. Josie Powell that was, prettiest deb in Dublin. Do you remember, Old Christmas night playing find the pin blindfold and thought reading?

MRS BREEN: (*Allowing herself to be held*)   You were the lion of the night. Love's old sweet song. After the parlour mystery games we sat under the mistletoe.

BLOOM: (*Pressing softly down on her palm*)   I took the splinter out of this hand.

MRS BREEN: (*Curving palm, breathing quickly*)   You're scalding! The left hand nearest the heart.

BLOOM: I can never forgive you for the choice you made. (*Hoarsely*) Woman, it's breaking me up!

MALE VOICES: (*Mocking in background*)   Up. Up. U.P. Up!

MRS BREEN: (*Holding palm up to BLOOM*)   Why didn't you kiss the spot to make it well?

BLOOM: (*Shocked*)   Molly's best friend! (*Hopeful*) Could you?

MRS BREEN: (*Offering a pigeon kiss*)   Hnhn. The answer is a lemon.

BAWD pulls at BLOOM'S arm again, then gives up in disgust.

BAWD: (*Stomping off*)   Jewman's melt!

BAWD's voice has broken spell. BLOOM turns to look after her and MRS BREEN retreats, surreal light fading. Stage fills again with street life as BLOOM begins to walk. SHAWLLED, DISHEVELLED WHORES stand about, calling.

WHORES: (*Different calls*)

> Are you going far, queer fellow?
>
> How's your middle leg?
>
> Eh, come here till I stiffen it for you.

A scratchy gramophone plays. HAGGLING SHEBEENKEEPER enters with the two SOLDIERS in tow.

PRIVATE CARR: (*Belching*)   Where's this bloody house of yours then?

SHEBEENKEEPER: (*Beckoning them*)   This way. Shilling a bottle of stout. Respectable women.

PRIVATE CARR: (*Laughs*)   What ho!

PRIVATE COMPTON: Say! What price the sergeant major?

PRIVATE CARR: He's my pal. I love old Bennett.

They stagger off after SHEBEENKEEPER. BLOOM shakes head, as WHORES watch from corners. One squats as if pissing drunkenly.

BLOOM: Wildgoose chase this. Disorderly houses. Second drink does it. What am I following him for? Still, he's the best of that lot in the hospital. He'll lose that cash. Relieving office down here. Dangerous.

TWO POLICEMEN approach him sternly, rain capes over their shoulders, bathed in surreal light. Both lay a hand on BLOOM.

FIRST WATCH: Caught in the act. Name and address.

BLOOM: (*Startled, trying to recover*) I have forgotten for the moment. Ah, yes! Dr Bloom, Leopold, dental surgeon. You have heard of von Bloom Pasha. Owns half Austria. Cousin. (*Takes off hat, saluting, card falls out. He picks it up hastily*) Allow me.

FIRST WATCH: (*Taking card, reading*) Henry Flower. No fixed abode. Unlawfully watching and besetting.

SECOND WATCH: An alibi. You are cautioned.

BLOOM: (*Produces Martha's crumpled flower*) This is the flower in question. It was given me by a man I don't know his name. (*Murmurs confidentially*) Lady in the case. (*Shoulders SECOND WATCH gently*) Dash it all. It's a way we gallants have in the navy. I'll introduce you, inspector. She's game. Do it in shake of a lamb's tail.

MARTHA appears at bedstead, veiled, clutching "Irish Times".

MARTHA: (*Tone of reproach*) Henry! Leopold! It is I, your Martha. Clear my name.

FIRST WATCH: (*Sternly*) Come to the station.

BLOOM: (*Scared, puts on hat, tries Masonic sign*) No, no, worshipful master. Mistaken identity.

MARTHA: (*Sobbing behind veil*) Breach of promise. My real name is Peggy Griffin. He wrote to me that he was miserable. I'll tell my brother, the Bective rugger fullback, on you.

BLOOM: (*Behind his hand*) She's drunk. The woman is inebriated.

SECOND WATCH: (*To BLOOM*) You ought to be well ashamed of yourself.

He pushes BLOOM backwards as URCHIN runs on, pushing a court dock on hidden wheels. BLOOM turns and collides with it, falling up the steps as URCHIN twirls him around and run off.

BLOOM: *(In declamatory pose)*   Gentlemen of the jury, let me explain. I am being made a scapegoat of. I am a respectable married man. My wife... I am the daughter of a most distinguished commander, Majorgeneral Tweedy, one of Britain's fighting men.

FIRST WATCH: Regiment.

BLOOM: *(Sweep of arms)*   The royal Dublins, the salt of the earth. I think I see some old comrades among you.

HECKLER: *(In shadows)*   Turncoat! Up the Boers!

FIRST WATCH: Profession or trade.

BLOOM: I follow a literary occupation. Author-journalist. In fact we are just bringing out a collection of prize stories. If you ring up...

MYLES CRAWFORD appears beside MARTHA with a quill between his teeth. He reaches into top of MARTHA'S hat to produce a telephone which he shouts into, silencing BLOOM.

CRAWFORD: Myles Crawford speaking. Editor *Freeman's Urinal* and *Weekly Arsewiper*. You which? Bluebags? Who writes? Is it Bloom?

FIRST WATCH: The King versus Bloom. Call the woman Driscoll, scullerymaid!

CRAWFORD and MARTHA retreat as MARY DRISCOLL appears at bedstead, carrying bucket and scouring-brush.

MARY DRISCOLL: I'm not a bad one, I bear a respectable character and was four months in my last place when I had to leave owing to his carryings on.

BLOOM: I treated you white. I gave you mementos, smart emerald garters far above your station. I took your part when you were accused of pilfering.

MARY DRISCOLL: *(Excitedly)*   As God is looking down on me I never laid a hand to them oysters!

FIRST WATCH: The offense complained of ?

MARY DRISCOLL: He surprised me, your honour, with a request for a safety pin. He held me and I was discoloured in four places as a result. And he interfered twict with my clothing.

BLOOM: She counterassaulted.

MARY DRISCOLL: (*Scornfully*) I had more respect for the scouring-brush. I remonstrated with him, your lord, and he remarked: Keep it quiet!

Background laughter.

SECOND WATCH: Order in the court! The accused will now make a bogus statement.

As BLOOM prepares to speak, BARRISTER in grey wig and stuffgown appears.

BARRISTER: (*Voice of pained protest*) My client is an infant, a poor foreign immigrant who started scratch as a stowaway. The trumped up misdemeanour was brought on by hallucination, such familarities as the alleged guilty occurrence being permitted in my client's native place, the land of the Pharaoh. There have been cases of shipwreck and somnambulism in my client's family. He himself, my lord, is a physical wreck from cobbler's weak chest. His submission is that he is of Mongolian extraction and irresponsible for his actions.

BLOOM tries to look dazed, then with shrug of oriental obeisance salutes court, pointing one finger heavenward.

I will not have any client of mine badgered by a pack of curs and laughing hyenas. The young person was treated by defendant as if she were his very own daughter. (*BLOOM reaches up to kiss BARRISTER'S hand*) The hidden hand is again at its old game. When in doubt persecute Bloom.

BLOOM: I can give best references. I have moved in the charmed circle of the highest ...Queens of Dublin Society

ACTRESS D in autocratic garb strides on from left.

ACTRESS D: Arrest him constable. He wrote to me an anonymous letter signed James Lovebirch. He said that he had seen from the gods my peerless globes as I sat in a box of the *Theatre Royal*. I deeply inflamed him, he said. He offered to send me through the post a work of fiction by Monsieur Paul de Kock, entitled *The Girl with the Three Pairs of Stays.*

ACTRESS B, equally richly dressed, has entered from right.

ACTRESS B: Also to me. He addressed me in several hand-writings, with fulsome compliments as a Venus in furs. He stated that it was his mission in life to urge me to defile the marriage bed, to commit adultery at the earliest possible opportunity.

ACTRESS D: Shame on him!

ACTRESS A clambers menacingly from under bed in full hunting costume, repeatedly striking hunting crop against her thigh.

ACTRESS A: Also me. This plebeian Don Juan observed me from behind a hackney car at the Phoenix park polo ground during the match All Ireland versus the Rest of Ireland. He sent me an obscene photograph, representing a partially nude senorita (his wife he assured me) practicing illicit intercourse with a muscular torero. He implored me to soil his letter in an unspeakable manner, to chastise him as he richly deserves, to give him a most vicious horsewhipping.

ACTRESS B AND D: (*Together approaching*)   Me too!

BLOOM: (*Expectantly as he squirms*)   I love the danger.

ACTRESS A: (*Raising crop in fury*)   I'll flay the pigeon-livered cur alive.

BLOOM: (*In alarm*)   Wait. I meant only the spanking idea.

ACTRESS A: (*Laughs derisively*)   Well, by the living God, you'll get the surprise of your life. You have lashed the dormant tigress in my nature into fury.

ACTRESS B: (*Vindictively*)   Thrash the mongrel within an inch of his life. Geld him. Vivisect him.

ACTRESS A: (*Swishes crop savagely*)   I'll dig my spurs in him up to the rowel, the well known cuckold.

BLOOM crouches in terror and URCHIN rushes on again, spinning dock round in circles. The ACTRESSES retreat smartly.

BOY: (*As NEWSBOY*)   Saint Patrick's Day Supplement of the Sacred Heart Messenger! Containing addresses of all the cuckolds in Dublin!

BLOOM is propelled to the front of stage to face audience. He raises head as if looking down line of faces.

BACKGROUND VOICES: Cuckoo! Cuckoo! Cuckoo!

FIRST WATCH: Call the jury.

BLOOM: Martin Cunningham, Simon Dedalus, Lenehan, M'Coy. But you all know me. You can't...

SECOND WATCH: Whereas Leoplod Bloom of no fixed abode is a wellknown forger, bawd and cuckold and a public nuisance to the citizens of Dublin...

JUDGE appears at bedstead in judicial garb, wearing Mosaic ramshorns.

JUDGE: (*Dons black cap*) Let him be taken, Mr Subsheriff, and detained in Mountjoy prison and there be hanged by the neck until he is dead and therein fail not at your peril or may the Lord have mercy on your soul.

FIRST WATCH: (*Calls*) Who will hang Judas Iscariot?

HANGMAN enters in bloodcoloured jerkin and tanner's apron, a rope on his shoulder as bells toll.

HANGMAN: (*To judge with sinister familiarity*) Hanging Harry, your Majesty. Five guineas a jugular. Neck or nothing.

BLOOM: (*Desperately*) Wait. Stop. Innocence. I was at a funeral.

FIRST WATCH: (*Pulling him from dock*) Liar!

The action is halted by the sight of PADDY DIGNAM, face ashen grey, who enters in brown decaying shroud.

DIGNAM: (*Hollow voice*) It is true. It was my funeral. (*Gasps all round*) I am Paddy Dignam's spirit. List, O list!

SECOND WATCH: (*Releases BLOOM and blesses himself*) How is that possible?

FIRST WATCH: It is not in the penny catechism.

DIGNAM: By metempsychosis. (*WATCH looks puzzled*) Spooks.

WATCH: (*Together*) Oh.

URCHIN silently wheels dock offstage. ACTOR D picks up a megaphone.

ACTOR D: (*Shouts loudly*) Dignam, Patrick T., deceased.

DIGNAM: (*Winces*) My masters' voice! (*Beseeching as he exits*) Pray for the repose of his soul.

Surreal lights die. Stage clears. Only street lights are left, dim, sordid.
ZOE HIGGINS (a young whore in sapphire slip) approaches BLOOM
who stares after vanished DIGNAN.

ZOE: (*Trying to get his attention*)   Are you looking for someone?
(*BLOOM looks at her*) He's in Mrs Cohen's with his friend. You might
go farther and fare worse. Mother Slipperslapper. (*Familiarly*) She's
on the job herself tonight with the vet, that pays for her son in Oxford.
(*Suspiciously*) You're not his father, are you?

BLOOM: Not I!

ZOE: (*Hand sliding over his left thigh*)   You both in black. Has
little mousey any tickles tonight? How's the nuts?

BLOOM: Off side.

ZOE: (*In sudden alarm*)   Wait, I can feel it.

BLOOM: Not likely.

Her hand slides into his left trouser pocket and brings out hard black
shrivelled potato. She looks at it and then him.

BLOOM: A talisman. Heirloom.

ZOE: (*Pocketing it greedily, linking his arm*)   Potato? For Zoe?
For keeps? For being so nice, eh? (*BLOOM draws back slightly, yet*
mechanically caresses her right breast) Have you a swaggerroot?

BLOOM: Rarely smoke dear. Cigar now and then. (*Lewdly*) The
mouth can be better engaged than with a cylinder of rank weed.

ZOE: (*Huffily*)   Go on. Make a stump speech out of it.

BLOOM looks towards back of stage which becomes bathed in surreal
light again as figures enter.

BLOOM: (*Impassionedly*)   Machines is the cry of these flying
Dutchmen or lying Dutchmen, laborsaving apparatuses,
manufactured monsters for mutual murder, hideous hobgoblins
produced by a horde of capitalistic lusts. The poor man starves while
they are grassing their royal mountain stags. But their reign is rover
for rever and ever...

Chimes sound from distant steeples. ROBED CITY COUNCILLOR
steps forward.

COUNCILLOR: Salute Leopold! Lord mayor of Dublin! Give
notice that the thoroughfare hitherto known as Cow Parlour be
henceforth designated Boulevard Bloom.

*Wild cheering. BLOOM moves from ZOE towards light where figures peer at him in wonder. Streamer bearing the legends "**Cead Mille Failte**" and "**Mah Ttob Melek Israel**" fall down.*

APRONED BLACKSMITH: For the Honour of God! Is that Bloom? He scarcely looks thirtyone.

ACTRESS A: (*Still in autocratic garb*) A classic face! He has the forehead of a thinker.

BISHOP OF DOWN AND CONNOR appears, framed by white halo. Others kneel.

BISHOP OF DOWN AND CONNOR: Will you to your power cause law and mercy to be executed in all your judgments?

BLOOM: (*Placing right hand on testicles*) So may the Creator deal with me.

BISHOP OF DOWN AND CONNOR: (*Making sign of cross*) God save Leopold the First!

OTHERS: (*Kneeling*) God save Leopold the First!

BLOOM: (*Handing up hand for silence*) My thanks, somewhat eminent bishop of Down and Connor. (*Declaims*) My beloved subjects, we have this day repudiated our former spouse and bestowed our royal hand upon the princess Selene, the splendour of night. I, Bloom, tell you ye shall now enter into the golden city which is to be the new Bloomusalem!

ACTOR D blows a ram's horn. The standard of Zion unfurls in the centre of the two existing banners.

ACTOR D: (*Lowering horn to shout*) The Court of Conscience is now open. His Most Catholic Majesty will now administer open air justice.

ACTOR C: (*Male voice*) What am I to do about my rates and taxes?

BLOOM: Pay them, my friend.

ACTOR C: (*In wonder*) So wise.

BISHOP OF DOWN AND CONNOR: (*Holding himself*) For bladder trouble?

ACTRESS D: What is the parallax of the subsolar ecliptic of Aldebaran?

BLOOM: (*Smiles as though explaining to child*)   K.II. (Tone changes to general address) I stand for the reform of municipal morals and the plain ten commandments. Union of all, jew, moslems and gentile. Three acres and a cow for all children of nature. Tuberculosis, lunacy and war must now cease. No more patriotism of bar spongers and dropsical impostors. Free money, free love and a free lay church in a free lay state.

ACTOR C: Free fox in a free hen roost.

BLOOM: Mixed races and mixed marriage.

ACTOR C: What about mixed bathing?

BISHOP OF DOWN AND CONNOR: He is an episcopalian seeking to overthrow our holy faith.

ACTRESS B: (*Shawled*)   You beast! You abominable person!

BLOOM: What railway opera is like a tramline in Gibraltar? The Rows of Casteele.

ACTOR C: That's Lenehan's joke. Plagiarist! Down with Bloom!

PREACHER: Fellow Christians and anti-Bloomites, the man called Bloom is from the roots of hell. (*General boos*) This vile hypocrite is the white bull mentioned in the Apocalypse. The stake faggots and the cauldron of boiling oil are for him. Caliban!

THE OTHERS: (*Rising violently*)   Lynch him! He's as bad as Parnell was.

BLOOM: (*Excitedly, over clamour*)   This is some midsummer madness. It was my brother Henry. He is my double. He lives in number 2 Dolphin's Barn. I call Dr Malachi Mulligan, sex specialist, to give medical testimony on my behalf.

MULLIGAN: (*Wearing motoring goggles*)   Dr Bloom is bi-sexually abnormal. He has recently escaped from Dr Eustace's private asylum for demented gentlemen. Born out of bedlock he is prematurely bald from self abuse, perversely idealistic in consequence, a reformed rake, and has metal teeth. I declare him to be *virgo intacta*.

BLOOM holds hat modestly over his genitals.

ACTOR A: (*Reads from long unfurling scroll*)   Professor Bloom is a finished example of the new womanly man. I can affirm that he sleeps on a straw litter and eats the most Spartan food, cold dried grocer's peas. I appeal for clemency in the name of the most sacred word our vocal organs have ever been called upon to speak. He is about to have a baby.

BLOOM: (*Bulging out stomach*)   O, I so want to be a mother.

General commotion and shrieks with ACTRESSES fainting. As BLOOM stands legs wide apart, URCHIN charges from behind him to swing beneath his legs and run off.

KNEELING CAST: (*Blessing themselves, kneeling*)

Kidney of Bloom, pray for us.

Canvasser for the Freeman, pray for us.

Charitable Mason, pray for us

Sweets of Sin, pray for us.

Their voices fade away with the surreal light until they are mute silhouettes and BLOOM is lit only by street light again.

ZOE: (*Pulling at his arm*)   Talk away till you're black in the face. Suppose you got up the wrong side of the bed or came too quick with your best girl.

BLOOM: (*Bitterly, glancing at her*)   Man and woman, love, what is it? A cork and bottle.

ZOE: (*Hurt, sulky*)   I hate a rotter that's insincere. Give a bleeding whore a chance.

BLOOM: (*Repentantly*)   I am very disagreeable. You are a necessary evil. Where are you from? London?

ZOE: (*Glibly*)   Hog's Norton where the pigs play the organs. I'm Yorkshire born. (*Stops his hand from feeling for her nipple*) I say, Tommy Tittlemouse. Stop that and begin worse. Have you cash for a short time? Ten shillings?

BLOOM: (*Smiles, nods slowly*)   More, houri, more.

ZOE: Are you coming into the music room to see our new pianola? Come and I'll peel off.

BLOOM: Somebody would be dreadfully jealous if she knew. (*Earnestly*) You know how difficult it is.

ZOE: (*Flattered*)   What the eye can't see the heart can't grieve for. Come. (*Takes hand, pulling him on*) Silence means consent.

He hesitates as intimate lights come up on sofas and pianola at back left of stage, then lets himself be led into lit arena. STEPHEN stands, playing pianola (on top of which lie his ashplant and hat). FLORRY

TALBOT (a blond whore in a tatterdemalion gown) lolls spreadeagle on sofa beside him, listening. LYNCH squats crosslegged on hearthrug, cap back to front, beating time with poker. KITTY RICKETTS (a pallid whore in navy costume, with sailor hat and doeskin gloves) perches on edge of pianola, swinging her leg.

KITTY: (*Behind her hand, indicating STEPHEN*)   Been   talking nonsense to his cap all night. (*LYNCH lifts her skirt and petticoat with the poker. She settles them down*) Respect yourself. (*She hiccups*) O, excuse!

ZOE: Your boy's thinking of you. Tie a knot on your shift.

KITTY bends her head, her boa sliding onto the floor. LYNCH lifts it with poker.

STEPHEN: (*Drunkenly to hat*)   What went forth to traverse not itself. God, the sun, Shakespeare, a commercial traveller, having itself traversed in reality, becomes that self. Damn that fellow's noise in the street. Self which it itself was ineluctably preconditioned to become. *Ecco!*

LYNCH: (*Mockingly*)   What a learned speech, eh?

ZOE: (*Briskly*)   He knows more than you have forgotten. Who has a fag as I'm here?

LYNCH: (*Tossing cigarette onto table*)   Here.

ZOE: (*Mock pride*)   Is that the way to hand the pot to a lady? (*She stretches to light cigarette from the gas. LYNCH with his poker lifts her slip to reveal legs bare from her garters up. She puffs calmly*) Can you see the beauty spot on my behind?

LYNCH: I'm not looking.

ZOE: (*Mock shame. Glancing at BLOOM*)   No? Would you suck a lemon?

STEPHEN: (*Tinkering at pianola, addressing hat*)   Play   with your eyes shut. Too much of this. I will arise and go to my. Must visit old Deasy or telegraph. Our interview has left a deep impression.

FLORRY: Sing us something. Love's old sweet song.

STEPHEN: No voice. Spirit is willing but the flesh is weak.

ZOE: Are you out of Maynooth? There was a priest down here two nights ago with his coat buttoned up. You needn't try to hide it, I says to him.

LYNCH: I hope you gave the good father a penance.

ZOE: (*Spouts smoke through nostrils*) He couldn't get a connection. Only, you know, a dry rush.

BLOOM: Poor man!

KITTY unpins hat and sets it down, patting her henna hair. LYNCH puts on her hat. She whips it off.

STEPHEN: (*Over shoulder to Zoe*) You would have preferred the fighting parson who founded the protestant error. But beware Antisthenes, the dog sage.

LYNCH: All one and the same God to her.

STEPHEN: (*Devoutly*) And Sovereign Lord of all things.

FLORRY: (*To Stephen*) I'm sure you are a spoiled priest. Or a monk.

LYNCH: He is. A Cardinal's son.

STEPHEN: Cardinal sin. (*Bows, blessing them*) I present, His Eminence, Simon Stephen Cardinal Dedalus, Primate of all Ireland.

There is a fall of light as if from a door opening offstage. The light stops just short of BLOOM'S feet.

ZOE: The devil is in that door.

BLOOM stares at huge silhouette of man filling patch of light. He takes out chocolate and nervously offers it to ZOE who tears it open, breaks off pieces and tosses them round.

BLOOM: (*To himself*) If it were Boylan? After Molly? Or because not? Or on the double? Go, go, go I conjure you, whoever you are.

The silhouette moves off. Bloom relaxes. Doorway light is suddenly filled by grotesquely huge silhouette of a woman who approaches. It is BELLA COHEN, a massive whoremistress in a threequarter ivory gown. Her eyes are deeply carboned. She stands in the light, with a folded fan.

BELLA: My word! I'm all of a mucksweat.

She glances at couples, then her eyes rest on BLOOM with hard insistence. She flicks fan open. It is multi-coloured and as it opens the light behind her takes on the same array of colours, spreading out, leaving STEPHEN and LYNCH frozen in semi-shade, but catching WHORES who run to crouch behind the fan.

BELLA: (*With whores peering out, sniggering*) Married, I see. And the missus is master. Petticoat government.

BLOOM: (*Looks down, sheepish grin*) That is so.

BELLA: We have met. You belong to the fan. Be mine.

BLOOM: (*Cowed*) Exuberant female. Enormously I desiderate your domination. I am exhaused, abandoned, no more young.

BELLA raises gown slightly to rest her shoe on a chair.

BELLA: (*Pointing fan downwards slowly*) Kneel! (*Stronger*) You must.

With desire and reluctance, BLOOM bends to tie up her lace.

ZOE: (*Kneeling with lips against the shoe*) Smell my hot goat hide.

BELLA: Hound of dishonour!

BLOOM: (*Infatuated*) Empress!

BELLA: Adorer of the adulterous rump! Dungdevourer! Down! On the hands down!

BLOOM: Truffles!

With piercing epileptic cry BLOOM sinks on all fours, snuffling, rooting at BELLA's feet.

BELLA: (*Grinding heel into BLOOM'S neck*) Bow, bond slave. Cheek me, I dare you.

WHORES come out from behind fan. BLOOM crawls behind them.

ZOE: (*Widening slip to screen him*) She's not here.

BLOOM: She's not here.

FLORRY: (*Hiding Bloom with gown*) She didn't mean it, Mr Bello. She'll be good, sir.

BELLA: (*Coaxingly*) Come, ducky dear. (*BLOOM puts head out timidly and BELLA drags him out*) I only want to correct you for your own good. How's that tender behind? (*Savagely*) The nose ring, the pliers, the hanging hook. (*Twists his arms viciously*) I'll make you remember me for the balance of your natural life.

BLOOM: (*Squeaks*) Don't be cruel, nurse! (*Screams*) O, it's hell itself!

BELLA: (*Shouts*)   Good, by the rumping jumping general! (*Slaps BLOOM'S face*) Hold him down, girls, till I squat on him.

ZOE: (*Eagerly coming to help*)   Yes. Walk on him! I will.

KITTY: (*As they hold and pinion Bloom*)   No, me. Lend him to me.

BLOOM: (*In agony*)   O! Monsters! Cruel one!

BELLA: (*Throwing leg astride Bloom as if he were a horse*)   Gee up! A cockhorse to Banbury cross. (*Squeezes testicles roughly*) Ho! Off we pop!

FLORRY: (*Pulls at BELLA*)   Let me on him now. I asked before you.

ZOE: (*Pulling at FLORRY*)   Me. Me.

BELLA: (*Contorts features, farts loudly*)   Take that! (*Stands up*) What you longed for has come to pass. Henceforth you are unmanned. You will shed your male garments, you understand, Ruby Cohen. (*Sternly*) The sins of your past are rising against you. Hundreds.

KITTY: (*Accusingly*)   In five public conveniences he wrote pencilled messages offering his nuptial partner to all strong membered males.

FLORRY: (*Accusingly*)   Did he not lie in bed gloating over a nauseous fragment of toilet paper presented to him by a nasty harlot, stimulated by gingerbread and a postal order?

BELLA: (*Imperiously as Bloom seems about to speak*)   Hold your tongue! By day you will swab out our pisspots with dress pinned up. Ay, and rinse them well, mind, or lap it up like champagne. Hop! You will dance attendance or I'll spank your barebot right well, miss, with the hairbrush. (*Chuckles*) My boys will be no end charmed to see you so ladylike. (*Sits on kneeling BLOOM'S back*) First, I'll have a go at you myself. (*Sinks fist through his closed legs*) There's fine depth for you! That give you a hardon, boys? (*Shoves fist towards WHORES to smell*) What offers?

ZOE: (*Bored male voice*)   Must be virgin. Good breath. Clean.

BELLA: (*Raps a gavel on BLOOM'S skull*)   Fourteen hands high. And quite easy to milk. So! What advance on two bob, gentlemen? (*Rises, pulling him by hair*) What else are you good for, an impotent thing like you? (*Her foot pokes at his testicles*) Up! Up! Manx cat! It's as limp as a boy of six's doing his pooly. (*Loudly*) Can you do a man's job?

BLOOM: Eccles Street...

BELLA: (*Sarcastically*) There's a man of brawn in possession there. Well for you if you had his weapon with knobs and lumps and warts all over it. Wait nine months, my lad! Holy ginger... (*Spits in contempt*) it's kicking and coughing up and down in her guts already!

BLOOM: (*Turns as if seeing MOLLY*) To drive me mad! Moll!

KITTY AND FLORRY: Rip Van Winkle! Rip Van Winkle!

Huge male shadow blocks light in doorway.

BLOOM: Let me go. I will return. I...

Silhouette moves. It is BOYLAN entering.

BOYLAN: (*Loudly*) Hello, Bloom! I have a little private business with your wife. (*Tossing him coin*) Here, to buy yourself a gin and splash.

BLOOM: Yes sir, thank you, Mr Boylan.

MOLLY'S VOICE: (*Towelled silhouette in doorway*) He ought to feel honoured. Come and dry me, darling. I'm in my bath.

BOYLAN: (*To BLOOM as he retreats towards silhouette*) Topping! You can apply your eye to the keyhole and play with yourself while I just go through her a few times.

BLOOM: Thank you, sir. Vaseline? May I bring two men chums to witness the deed?

FLORRY: (*Jumping on sofa, peering in excitement*) Yumyum. O, he's carrying her round the room doing it! Ride a cock horse.

BLOOM: (*Wildly, as if with eye to keyhole*) Show! Hide! Plough her! More! Shoot!

WHORES clap once on word "shoot". BLOOM'S head drops. Silhouettes vanish.

I will... (*Weakly*) shoot.

BELLA: Too late. You are down and out, old bean.

BLOOM: Justice! All Ireland versus one! Has nobody...?

BELLA: (*Contempt*) Die and be damned if you have any sense of decency. (*Phlegmy laugh*) We'll manure you, Mr Flower! Byby, Poldy! Baby, Papli!

BLOOM, broken, sobs. WHORES move backwards to their original positions when BELLA entered.

BLOOM: (*To himself*) Fraility thy name is marriage. The nymph above our bed. Unseen, one summer eve, I kissed her in four places. What has she looked down on? Soiled personal linen, that antiquated commode Molly broke because of a crack and want of glue. Enemas I have administered under her gaze. Up the fundament. With Hamilton Long's syringe, the ladies' friend.

KITTY: (*To Florry*) Show us one of them cushions..

FLORRY: (*Taking one from under her backside*) Here. From a hot place.

LYNCH: (*Catching it in mid-flight*) Whew! Piping hot!

BLOOM: (*Rising to stand as when BELLA entered*) That's broken the spell. I have sixteen years of black slave labour behind me. Fool someone else, not me.

Surreal light dies. BELLA opens fan again. It is plain.

BELLA: (*Repeats*) Married, I see.

BLOOM: (*Composed, regards her*) Mutton dressed as lamb and long in the tooth.

BELLA: (*Contemptuously*) You're not game, in fact.

BLOOM: (*Just as contemptuously*) Clean your nailless middle finger first.

BELLA: I know you, canvasser! Dead cod! (*Turns to piano*) Which of you was playing the dead march from *Saul?*

ZOE: Me. (*Bangs out chords on pianola, glancing back*) Eh? Who's making love to my sweeties?

BLOOM: (*Gently, approaching Zoe*) Give me back that potato, will you? (*With feeling*) It is nothing, but still a relic of poor mamma.

ZOE: Here. (*Hauls up slip, unrolls potato from top of her stocking*) Those that hides knows where to find.

BELLA: (*Frowns, moving to pianola*) Here. This isn't a musical peepshow. Who's paying here?

STEPHEN: (Fumbles in pocket for banknote with exaggerated politeness) Madam, if you allow me. (*Vaguely indicates Lynch and Bloom*) We are all in the same sweepstake. *Dans ce bordel òu tenons nostre état.*

LYNCH: (*Calls from hearth*)   Dedalus! Give her your blessing for me.

STEPHEN: Gold. She has it.

BELLA: (*Looks at money, then at whores*)   Do you want three girls. It's ten shillings here.

STEPHEN: A hundred thousand apologies. (*Fumbles again, hands her more money*) My sight is somewhat troubled.

WHORES rush to table where BELLA counts money while STEPHEN talks to himself in monosyllables. LYNCH clasps KITTY'S waist. BLOOM joins babbling voices. ZOE breaks free, lifts pettigown and folds half sovereign into top of her stocking.

ZOE: Hard earned on the flat of my back.

LYNCH: (*Lifting KITTY from table*)   Come!

KITTY: Wait!

She reaches back for coins, then lets LYNCH carry her to sofa.

BELLA: No more drink, it's long after eleven.

STEPHEN: The fox crew, the cocks flew,

The bells in heaven

Were striking eleven.

'Tis time for her poor soul

To get out of heaven.

BLOOM: (*Quietly placing money before BELLA*)   Allow   me. (*Takes pound note*) Three times ten. We're square.

BELLA: (*Admiringly*)   You're such a sly boots, old cocky.

ZOE: Him? Deep as a draw well.

LYNCH kisses KITTY. BLOOM brings pound to STEPHEN.

BLOOM: (*Quietly*)   This is yours. (*STEPHEN fumbles at pocket, scattering handful of coins*) You had better hand over that cash to me to take care of. (*STEPHEN hands him coins which he counts*) I don't answer for what you may have lost.

STEPHEN: Doesn't matter a rambling damn. (*To LYNCH*) Cigarette, please. (*LYNCH tosses him one*) And so Georgina Johnson is dead and married. (*Strikes match, tries to light it with enigmatic melancholy*) Married.

ZOE: It was a commercial traveller married her.

KITTY: (*Nods*) Mr Lambe from London.

STEPHEN: (*Cigarette slips from fingers*) Lamb of London, who takest away the sins of our world.

BLOOM: (*Picking up cigarette, throwing it away*) Don't smoke. You ought to eat. (*To Zoe*) You have nothing?

ZOE: Is he hungry? (*Takes STEPHEN'S hand*) Blue eyed beauty, I'll read your hand. (*Looks from palm into eyes*) Mars, that's courage.

LYNCH: Sheet lightning courage. Who taught you palmistry?

ZOE: Ask my ballocks that I haven't got. (*To STEPHEN*) I see it in your face. (*Examines palm*) What day were you born?

STEPHEN: (*Murmurs*) Thursday. Today.

ZOE: Thursday's child has far to go. (*Traces lines on his hand*) You'll meet with a... (*Abruptly*) I won't tell you what's not good for you.

BLOOM: (*Detaches her fingers from STEPHEN, offers his own palm*) More harm than good. Here. Read mine.

BELLA: (*Turning up BLOOM'S hand*) Show. Knobby knuckles, for the women.

ZOE: (*Peering at BLOOM'S palm*) Gridiron. Travels beyond the sea and marry money.

BLOOM: Wrong.

ZOE: (*Quickly*) Short little finger. Henpecked husband. That wrong?

STEPHEN: Et exaltabuntur cornua iusti. Queens lay with prize bulls.

BELLA: (*Warning*) None of that here. Come to the wrong shop.

LYNCH: Let him alone. He's back from Paris.

ZOE: (*Runs to STEPHEN and links him*) O go on! Give us some parleyvoo.

STEPHEN puts on hat, hands outspread, with painted smile.

STEPHEN: (*Gabbles, with marionette jerks*) Thousand places of entertainment to expenses your evenings with lovely ladies who arrive full of modesty then disrobe and squeal loud to see vampire debauch nun very fresh young. (*Cracks tongue*) *Ho, la la! Ce pif qu'il a!*

LYNCH: Vive le vampire!

WHORES: Bravo! Parleyvoo! (*Laughing*) Encore! Encore!

STEPHEN: (*Remembering dream*) Mark me. It was here. I remember. Dream. Street of harlots. Where's the red carpet spread?

BLOOM: (*Approaching STEPHEN*) Look . . .

STEPHEN: No, I flew. My foes beneath me. And ever shall be. World without end. *Pater*! Free!

BLOOM: I say, look...

STEPHEN: Break my spirit, will he! Hola! Hilly ho!

Offstage, PRIVATES CARR and COMPTON drunkenly sing "My Girl's a Yorkshire Girl".

Hark! Our friend, noise in the street!

ZOE: (*Claps hands*) Stop! That's me. Dance! Dance! (*Runs to pianola*) Who has twopence?

LYNCH: (*Handing her coins*) Here.

STEPHEN: (*Cracking fingers impatiently*) Quick! Where's my augur's rod?

He runs to pianola and takes ashplant, beating foot in tripudium. ZOE turns drumhandle and drops pennies in slot. Coloured lights start forth as drum turns, purring in low hesitation waltz.

ZOE: (*Twirls around*) Dance. Who'll dance?

Pianola, with changing, glowing lights, plays prelude to "My Girl's a Yorkshire Girl". STEPHEN throws ashplant on table and seizes ZOE around waist and with exaggerated grace, begins to waltz her around the room.

FLORRY: (*Singing*) Two young fellows were talking about their girls, girls, girls, sweethearts they'd left behind...

ZOE: (*Freeing herself, drops onto chair*) I'm giddy.

STEPHEN seizes FLORRY and dances.

KITTY: (*Jumps up*) O, they played that on the hobbyhorses at the Mirus bazaar!

She runs to STEPHEN who leaves FLORRY brusquely to seize her.

ZOE: (*Singing*)

> My girl's a Yorkshire girl.
>
> Yorkshire through and through.
>
> (*Seizing Florry and waltzing her*) Come on all!

STEPHEN wheels KITTY into LYNCH'S arms, snatches ashplant and takes the floor. All whirl and waltz, BLOOM included, STEPHEN moving out of control.

ZOE: Though she's a factory lass

> And wears no fancy clothes.
>
> Baraabum.
>
> Yet I've a sort of a
>
> Yorkshire relish for
>
> My little Yorkshire rose.

STEPHEN: (*Shouts*) Dance of death, Father.

ZOE and FLORRY stop dancing to stare at him. FLORRY steps back. STEPHEN whirls giddily, then stops dead, staring at ZOE who is hit by spotlight which makes her flesh seem ashen. A green rill of bile starts to trickle from her mouth.

ZOE: (*Becoming MOTHER'S GHOST*) I was once the beautiful May Goulding. I am dead.

STEPHEN: (*Horrorstruck*) What bogeyman's trick is this?

Dancers stop, staring at STEPHEN, noticing nothing about ZOE.

ZOE: (*As MOTHER*) All must go through it, Stephen. You too. Time will come.

STEPHEN: (*Choking with fright and remorse*) They said I killed you, mother. Cancer did it, not I. Destiny.

KITTY: (*Points to STEPHEN*) Look! He's white. Why's he staring like that?

ZOE: (*As MOTHER*) I pray for you in my other world. O my firstborn, when you lay in my womb.

FLORRY: (*Alarmed*) Zoe! Why's he looking at you like that?

BLOOM: Giddy. Open a window.

ZOE: (*As MOTHER*) Repent! O, the fire of hell!

STEPHEN: (*Chanting*)   The ghoul! Hyena! Raw head and bloody bones!

ZOE: (*As MOTHER*)   Beware! (*Points a withered right arm slowly towards STEPHEN'S breast*) God's hand!

STEPHEN: (*Strangled with rage*)   Shite!

BLOOM: (*Looking around*)   How do you open this window?

FLORRY: Give him some cold water. Wait. (*Exits*)

ZOE: (*As Mother, wrings hands, moaning desperately*)   O Sacred Heart of Jesus, save him from hell!

STEPHEN: No! Break my spirit if you can! I'll bring you all to heel!

STEPHEN lifts the ashplant to smash chandelier, killing spotlight and releasing ZOE who puts hands to her face and turns away.

BLOOM: Stop!

LYNCH: (*Seizes STEPHEN'S hand*)   Here! Don't run amok!

STEPHEN, abandoning ashplant, flees offstage.

BELLA: (*Screams*)   Police! After him!

LYNCH, KITTY and ZOE stampede off. BELLA seizes BLOOM'S coattail.

KITTY: (*Offstage*)   He's down there. There's something up!

BELLA: Who pays for the lamp? Ten shillings.

BLOOM: (*Snatches up ashplant*)   Haven't you lifted enough off him?

BELLA: (*Loudly*)   None of your tall talk. (*Shrinks as BLOOM lifts ashplant*) Jesus! Don't!

BLOOM: To show you how he hit the paper. There's not a sixpenceworth of damage done.

BELLA: Do you want me to call the police?

BLOOM: He's a Trinity student. Gentlemen that pay the rent. (*Makes a Masonic sign*) Know what I mean. You don't want a scandal.

BELLA: (*Angrily*)   Disgrace him, I will (*Shouts*) Zoe!

BLOOM: (*Urgently*)   And if it were your own son in Oxford! (*Warningly*) I know.

BELLA: (*Almost speechless*)   Who are you incog?

ZOE: (*Appearing*)   There's a row on.

BLOOM: (*Throws coin on the table*)   That's for the lamp. Where? (*Turns to follow ZOE, then stops, alarmed*) Corny Kelleher coming in here with two fellows.

He puts up a hand to hide his face and rushes offstage left as, from right, PRIVATES CARR and COMPTON with GIRL, STEPHEN, URCHIN, and BAWD enter in tense shouting ruck.

STEPHEN: (*To soldiers, with elaborate gestures*)   You are my guests. The uninvited. History to blame.

PRIVATE CARR: (*To GIRL*)   Was he insulting you while me and him was having a piss?

KITTY: (*Arriving with LYNCH*)   The girl's telling lies. He was in Mrs Cohen's with us.

GIRL: I was in company with the soldiers and the young man ran up behind me. But I'm faithful to the man that's treating me though I'm only a shilling whore.

STEPHEN: (*Sees LYNCH, points to himself and others*)   Poetic. Neopoetic.

PRIVATE COMPTON: Biff him one, Harry.

PRIVATE CARR: (*Cap awry, advancing on STEPHEN*)   Say, how would it be, governor, if I was to bash in your jaw?

STEPHEN: Very unpleasant. Personally, I detest action. (*To GIRL*) What is the trouble precisely?

BLOOM: (*Pushing through crowd, plucking STEPHEN'S sleeve*) Come now, professor, that carman is waiting.

STEPHEN: (*Disengages himself*)   Eh? I'm not afraid of what I can talk to if I see his eye. (*Slight stagger, laughs emptily*) My centre of gravity is displaced. Let us sit somewhere and discuss. Struggle for life is the law of existence but modern philirenists, notably the tsar amd the king of England, have invented arbitration. (*Taps brow*) But in here it is I must kill the priest and the king.

PRIVATE CARR: (*Menacingly*)   What's that you're saying about my king?

STEPHEN: (*Nervous, friendly*)   I understand your point of view, though I have no king myself. But this is the point. You die for your country, suppose. (*Places arm on PRIVATE CARR*) Not that I wish it for you. But I say: Let my country die for me. Up to the present it has done so. I don't want it to die. Long live life! (*Falls back a pace*) Come somewhere and we'll... What was that girl saying?

PRIVATE COMPTON: Eh, Harry, give him a kick in the knackers.

BLOOM: (*To PRIVATES, softly*) He doesn't know what he's saying. He's a gentleman, a poet.

STEPHEN: (*Nods, laughing*) Gentleman, patriot, scholar and judge of impostors.

PRIVATE COMPTON: We don't give a bugger who he is. What are you saying about my king?

STEPHEN: (*Throws up hands, goes to move off*) O this is too monotonous!

GIRL: (*Shrilly*) Stop them from fighting!

BLOOM: (*Terrified*) He said nothing. A pure misunderstanding.

GIRL: (*Thrilled*) They re going to fight! For me!

PRIVATE CARR: (*Loosening belt*) I'll wring the neck of any fucking bastard says a word against my bleeding fucking king.

BLOOM: (*Runs to Lynch*) Can't you get him away?

LYNCH: He likes dialectic, the universal language. (*Starts to drag KITTY away*) Get him away, you. He won't listen to me.

STEPHEN: (*Points*) Exit Judas.

BLOOM: (*To STEPHEN*) Come along before worse happens. Here's your stick.

STEPHEN: Stick, no. Reason.

GIRL: (*Pulling PRIVATE CARR*) Come on. I forgive him for insulting me.

BLOOM: (*Over STEPHEN'S shoulder*) Yes, go. You see he's incapable.

PRIVATE CARR: (*Breaks loose*) I'll insult him.

He rushes towards STEPHEN and strikes him in the face. STEPHEN collapses and lies prone, face up as crowd push and shove.

SHAWLLED HAG: (*Entering*) What call had the redcoat to strike the gentleman and he under the influence?

BAWD: (*Grabbing at her*)   Hasn't the soldier a right to go with his girl?

BLOOM: (*Shoves women back as they fight*)   Get   back,   stand back!

FIRST WATCH enters.

FIRST WATCH: What's wrong here?

GIRL: (*With expectation*)   Is he bleeding?

BLOOM: (*Pushing people back*)   Leave him to me. I can easily...

FIRST WATCH: Who are you? Do you know him?

PRIVATE CARR: (*Lurches towards WATCH*)   He   insulted   my lady friend.

BLOOM: (*Angrily*)   You hit him without provocation. I'm a witness. Constable, take his regimental number.

FIRST WATCH: I don't want your instructions.

PRIVATE COMPTON: (*Pulling comrade*)   Here,   bugger   off, Harry. Or Bennett'll have you in the lockup.

PRIVATE CARR: (*Staggering as he is pulled away*)   God   fuck old Bennett. I don't give a shit for him.

FIRST WATCH: (*Taking out his notebook*)   What's his name?

BLOOM: (*Peering over crowd*)   I just see a car there. if you give me a hand, sergeant...

FIRST WATCH: Name and address.

CORNY KELLEHER appears among bystanders.

BLOOM: Kelleher! The very man! (*Whispers*) Simon Dedalus' son. A bit sprung.

KELLEHER: (*To WATCH*)   That's all right. I know him. Won a bit on the races. *Throwaway.* (*Laughs*) Do you follow me?

FIRST WATCH: (*To CROWD*)   Move on out of that.

CROWD exit slowly, muttering.

KELLEHER: (*Nudges WATCH*)   Leave   it   to   me,   sergeant. (*Laughs, shakes head*) We were often as bad ourselves, ay or worse. (*Lilts*) With my tooraloom tooraloom tooraloom tooraloom. What?

FIRST WATCH: (*Laughs genially*) Ah, sure we were too. All right, Mr Kelleher. Good night.

BLOOM: (*Shakes hands with WATCH, mumbles confidentially*) Father is a highly respected citizen. Just a little wild oats, you understand.

FIRST WATCH: That's all right, sir. (*Salutes*) Night, gentlemen.

Exits with slow heavy tread.

BLOOM: Providential you came on the scene. You have a car?

KELLEHER: (*Laughs, points over shoulder*) Two commercials that were standing fizz in Jammet's and were on for a go with the jolly girls. So I landed them up on Behan's car and down to nighttown.

BLOOM: I was just going home by Gardiner street when...

KELLEHER: (*Laughs*) Sure they wanted me to join in with the mots. No, by God, says I. Not for old stagers like myself and yourself. (*Leers*) Thanks be to God we have it in the house what, eh?

BLOOM: (*Tries to laugh*) Yes. Matter of fact I was just visiting an old friend there, Virag...

KELLEHER: (*Bends and calls to STEPHEN*) Eh! (*To BLOOM*) He's covered with shavings anyhow. Take care they didn't lift anything off him.

BLOOM: I have his money and his hat here and stick.

KELLEHER: Ah well, he'll get over it. I'll shove along. (*Laughs*) I've a rendezvous in the morning. Burying the dead. Safe home!

BLOOM: Good night. I'll just wait and take him along in a few...

KELLEHER exits.

Eh! Mr Dedalus! (*Bends again and hesitating, brings mouth near STEPHEN'S face*) Stephen! Stephen!

STEPHEN: (*Groans*) Who? Black panther vampire. (*Sighs, mumbling thickly*)

      Who... drive... Fergus now.

      And pierce... wood's woven shade...

BLOOM: Poetry. Well educated. (*Bends to undo STEPHEN'S waistcoat and brushes his clothes lightly*) Wood shavings. One pound seven. Not hurt anyhow. (*Listens*) What!

STEPHEN: (*Murmurs*)

> ...shadows... the woods.

> ...white breast...dim...

He stretches out, sighs, curls up. BLOOM, holding hat and ashplant, stands guard over him.

BLOOM: (*Softly*)   Face reminds me of his poor mother. The deep white breast. Ferguson, I think I caught. Some girl. Best thing could happen him... (*Murmurs*)...swear that I will always hail, never reveal, any part or parts, art or arts...(*Pause*) in the rough sands of the sea... a cable tow's length from the shore... where the tide ebbs... and flows...

Thoughtfully, BLOOM turns to back of stage where RUDY appears in white light. His suit has diamond and ruby buttons. His left hand holds a ivory cane with violet bowknot. A white lambkin peeps from his waistcoat pocket. He smiles, kissing the book he is reading.

BLOOM: (*Softly, wonderstruck*)   Rudy!

RUDY gazes unseeing into BLOOM'S eyes and continues reading, kissing, smiling. Lights fade.

SCENE FIVE

Cabman's Shelter, Butt Bridge,   **12.40 a.m.**

Over mellow, sleepy music softer lights return. BLOOM helps an unsteady STEPHEN to his feet, brushing him down, handing him hat and ashplant.

BLOOM: (*Hand on shoulder*)   Coffee... something to eat... There's a cabman's shelter at Butt Bridge. Do you think you can walk? (*STEPHEN yawns, dazed*) You were almost arrested I have to tell you, only a friend of your father's turned up. All your drinking friends seemed to abandon you back at Westland Row station, except for (*Looks around for LYNCH*) one...

STEPHEN: And that one was Judas.

BLOOM: (*Hand on STEPHEN'S elbow*)   Try walking.

LORD JOHN CORLEY, in ragged coat, shuffles towards them and beckons.

BLOOM: He seems to be saluting you.

A reluctant BLOOM stays back, watching.

CORLEY: You know me... through your father... Corley, Lord John they call me. Would you know of anything going? I wouldn't ask, only, God knows, I'm on the rocks.

STEPHEN: There'll be a job tomorrow in a boy's school in Dalkey. Mr Garrett Deasy. You may mention my name.

CORLEY: (*Nervous laugh*)   Ah, God, sure I couldn't teach in a school, man.

STEPHEN: (*Searching for coins*)   Just... pennies left... I think...

CORLEY: (*Watching carefully*)   Those are half crowns, man.

STEPHEN looks at them in surprise, then hands him one.

CORLEY: You're a gentleman. (*Glances at BLOOM*) Who's that with you? I saw him a few times with Boylan the billsticker. You might put a good word in for me.

He exits. BLOOM rejoins STEPHEN.

STEPHEN: (*Half laugh*)   He asked me to ask you to ask somebody called Boylan to give him a job as a sandwichman. (*Pockets remaining coins*) I daresay he needs money to sleep somewhere.

BLOOM: Where will you sleep yourself? I don't mean to presume to dictate to you but why did you leave your father's house?

STEPHEN: To seek misfortune.

BLOOM: He takes great pride, quite legitimately, in you. You could go back.

STEPHEN does not reply. SHELTER-KEEPER, SAILOR, paper reading JARVEY and pipe-smoking VETERAN sit, front right stage, shoulders hunched, tired.

Here's the cabman's shelter.

STEPHEN and BLOOM stoop and survey men. BLOOM motions STEPHEN to sit and approaches SHELTER-KEEPER.

Coffee. And something to eat. (*Looks*) A bun. All you have?

KEEPER hands him coffee and mauled bun.

SAILOR: (*To STEPHEN as BLOOM returns*)   Murphy's   the name. A seadog. And what might yours be?

STEPHEN: Dedalus.

SAILOR: You know Simon Dedalus?

STEPHEN: I've heard of him.

SAILOR: He's Irish. All Irish.

STEPHEN: All too Irish.

BLOOM urges coffee and bun on STEPHEN.

SAILOR: (*Addressing company*)   I seen him shoot two eggs off two bottles at fifty yards over his shoulder (*Shuts eye, screws up features and gestures*) Pom! (*Dramatic pause to aim*) Pom! (*Lowers finger*) I seen him do that in Hengler's Royal Circus in Stockholm.

BLOOM: (*Quietly to STEPHEN*)   Curious coincidence.

SAILOR: (*To JARVEY*)   You don't happen to have such a thing as a spare chaw about you, do you?

JARVEY shakes head as KEEPER finds a die of plug which is passed down to him.

KEEPER: You must have seen a fair share of the world.

SAILOR: I sailed the Red Sea, China, South America, the Dardanelles. (*Begins to chew plug*) I seen icebergs plenty, growlers. I seen Russia. *Gospodi pomilooy.* That's how the Russians prays.

JARVEY: (*Not looking up from paper*)   You seen queer sights, don't be talking.

SAILOR: I seen a crocodile bite an anchor same as I chew this quid. (*Bites ferociously*) And I saw maneaters in Peru that eats the livers of horses. I see a Chinaman that had little pills like putty and every one he put in the water opened into something different. A ship, a horse, a flower. (*Looks around, suspecting others disbelieve him*) And I seen a man killed in Trieste by an Italian chap. Knife in the back. Like that. (*Produces vicious claspknife which he holds in striking position*) In a knocking shop. *Prepare to meet your God*, says he. Chunk! Into his back up to the butt.

Looks around at the wary faces to see who disbelieves him now, then stashes knife away.

BLOOM: (*Breaking slightly tense silence*)   Have you seen the rock of Gibraltar?

SAILOR makes a glimace that could mean yes or no, then spits.

What year would that be? Can you recall the boats?

SAILOR: (*Suddenly tired, clamping up*)   I'm sick of all them rocks in the sea, and boats and ships.

SAILOR sits as haggard-looking PROSTITUTE briefly peers in at them, plying her trade. Only SAILOR gives her a second glance.

BLOOM: (*To STEPHEN*)   It beats me how an unfortunate creature like that, reeking of disease, can be barefaced enough...

STEPHEN: In this country people sell much more than she ever had and do a roaring trade. Fear not them that sell the body but have not power to buy the soul.

BLOOM: Have a shot at that coffee now. (*STEPHEN takes sip with little enthusiasm. BLOOM pushes bun towards him*) You ought to eat. You would feel a different man.

STEPHEN: Liquids, I can eat.

BLOOM: (*Glancing at SAILOR*)   Our friends stories are like himself. Mind you I'm not saying it's all pure invention. That stab in the back is quite in keeping with those Italianos. Spaniards are the same, passionate temperaments. My wife is, so to speak, Spanish, half, that is technically. Born in Gibraltar. She has the Spanish type.

SAILOR: (*To STEPHEN, rising*)   Let me cross your bows, mate.

He passes STEPHEN and sleeping JARVEY, stoops and looks around, possibly for prostitute, then turns his back and mimes urinating.

KEEPER: (*Almost to himself*)   The day of reckoning is coming.

JARVEY: (*Looking up from sleep*)   How's that?

KEEPER: For England. She's toppling already and we'll be her downfall, Ireland, her Achilles heel.

VETERAN: (*Removing pipe for first time*)   Who's the best troops in the empire? And the best admirals and generals?

JARVEY: The Irish Catholic peasant.

KEEPER: (*Hotly*)   I care nothing for any empire and there's no Irishman worth his salt would serve one.

ACT TWO

A row is stopped by return of SAILOR who whips out knife.

SAILOR: Seen Indians. (*Makes swipe across his chest*) Cuts off their diddies when they can't bear no more children.

He puts knife away and sits down. BLOOM glances at KEEPER.

BLOOM: (*To STEPHEN*)   The little Irelanders. One of them attacked me today. He called me a jew. So I told him his God was a jew too. That was one for him. Am I not right? (*STEPHEN nods noncommitally*) I resent violence or intolerance in any shape or form. A revolution must come on the due installments plan. All these wretched quarrels, suppose to be about honour and flags. It's money at the back of everything, greed and jealousy. They accuse... (*Whispers word*) jews. Not a vestige of truth. History proves Spain decayed when the Inquisition hounded them out and England prospered when that ruffian Cromwell imported them. Because they're practical. I'm as good an Irishman as him and I want to see all classes and creeds, being able to live well, if they work.

STEPHEN: (*Attention back to BLOOM on last words*)   Count me out.

BLOOM: (*Quickly*)   I mean work in the widest sense. Also literary labour. Writing for the newspapers. Both the brain and the brawn belong to Ireland.

STEPHEN: (*Half laugh*)   You suspect that I may be important because I belong to Ireland. But I suspect that Ireland must be important because it belongs to me.

BLOOM: (*Confused*)   What belongs? Excuse me.

STEPHEN: (*Sighing, pushing coffee aside*)   We can't change the country. Let us change the subject.

BLOOM flicks through JARVEY'S tattered newspaper.

BLOOM: (*Reading*)   "This morning the remains of the late Mr Patrick Dignam, a most popular and genial personality, were interred in Glasnevin. The mourners included Patk. Dignan (son), Martin Cunningham, Simon Dedalus," (*Voice drops*) "L. Boom," (*Looks at STEPHEN*) "Stephen Dedalus, B.A."

STEPHEN: (*Yawns*)   Is Garrett Deasy's first epistles to the Hebrews in?

While STEPHEN reads BLOOM produces a faded photograph, which he places down when STEPHEN lifts his eyes.

102

BLOOM: Do you consider that a Spanish type? My wife the prima donna. Taken a few years since.

BLOOM looks around, not wishing to intrude on STEPHEN'S examination of photograph.

STEPHEN: *(Handing it back)* A handsome picture.

BLOOM: *(Putting picture away)* At what o'clock did you dine?

STEPHEN: Some time yesterday... the day before yesterday.

BLOOM: It's rather stuffy in here. You just come with me and talk things over. My diggings are quite close. *(Rising)* The only thing is to walk, then you'll feel a different man. *(Holds out hand as STEPHEN rises, unsteadily)* It's not far. Lean on me.

STEPHEN: *(Standing, allowing arm to be taken)* Yes.

BLOOM: *(Begins to walk)* My wife would have the greatest pleasure in making your acquaintance. Come.

They take a step and light changes, freezing them.

SCENE SIX

Ithaca. Cabman's Shelter to Eccles street,   **1 a.m.**

SAILOR and JARVEY rise behind STEPHEN and BLOOM who take a step after each question.

SAILOR: Of what did Bloom and Stephen deliberate during their walk?

JARVEY: Music, literature, friendship, woman, prostitution, the Irish nation, the past day, Stephen's collapse.

KEEPER and VETERAN rise.

KEEPER: Did Bloom discover common factors?

VETERAN: Both professed disbelief in many orthodox religious and national doctrines. Both admitted the alternately stimulating and obtunding influence of heterosexual magnetism.

SAILOR: Were their views on some points divergent?

JARVEY: Stephen dissented openly from Bloom's views on the importance of dietary and civic selfhelp while Bloom dissented tacitly from Stephen's views on the eternal affirmation of the spirit of man in literature.

ACTRESSES A and B enter.

ACTRESS A: In Eccles Street, what was Bloom's stratagem upon discovering he had no key?

BLOOM crouches. ACTRESSES D and C enter, carrying lit candles.

ACTRESS B: He climbed the railings and crouched in preparation for the fall.

SAILOR: What image did Stephen shortly perceive?

ACTRESSES A and B kneel, removing boots of unaware BLOOM.

JARVEY: A man holding a candle.

KEEPER: What mark of hospitality did Bloom show his guest?

VETERAN: He poured into two teacups two level spoonfuls of Epps soluble cocoa.

ACTRESS C: How did the guest receive this hospitality?

ACTRESS D: He accepted it seriously as they drank in jocoserious silence Epps's massproduct.

KEEPER: What separating forces did Bloom find between them?

VETERAN: Name, age, race, creed.

SAILOR: Did either openly allude to their racial difference?

JARVEY: Neither.

KEEPER: What proposal did Bloom make to Stephen?

VETERAN: To pass in repose the night intervening on an extemporised cubicle immediately adjacent to the sleeping apartment of his host and hostess.

ACTRESS D: What various advantages would or might have resulted from a prolongation of such extemporisation?

JARVEY: For the guest: security of domicile.

VETERAN: For the host: rejuvenation of intelligence.

ACTRESS C: For the hostess: disintegration of obsession with Boylan, acquisition of correct Italian pronunciation.

KEEPER: Was the proposal of asylum accepted?

VETERAN: Promptly, inexplicably, with amicability, gratefully it was declined.

ACTRESSES blow candles out. BLOOM and STEPHEN move forward, gazing in awe upwards as backdrop changes to rich nightscape lit by stars.

KEEPER: What spectacle confronted them when they emerged silently into the penumbra of the garden?

VETERAN: The heaventree of stars hung with humid nightblue fruit.

ACTRESS C: What luminous sign attracted Bloom's, who attracted Stephen's gaze?

ACTRESS D: The light of a paraffin oil lamp denoting the mystery of an invisible person, his wife Marion (Molly) Bloom.

Heads high, their hands are lowered in stance of urinating.

SAILOR: Were they indefinitely silent?

JARVEY: At Stephen's suggestion, at Bloom's instigation, both urinated, gazes elevated to the projected luminous shadow.

STEPHEN backs away from BLOOM to where RUDY waits to take his hand, leading him off.

KEEPER: Alone, after Stephen's departure, what did Bloom feel?

VETERAN: The cold of interstellar space, the incipient intimations of proximate dawn.

ACTRESS C: Did he remain?

ACTRESS D: With deep inspiration he returned, reclosing the door.

SAILOR and KEEPER tilt motionless BLOOM, taking his weight, moving backwards. They stop at edge of bed. ACTRESSES unclothe BLOOM, pulling long nightshirt over his head.

VETERAN: How did Bloom enter the bed?

ACTRESS D: With circumspection: prudently: lightly, the less to disturb: reverently, the bed of conception and of birth, of consummation and breach of marriage, of sleep and of death.

ACTRESS B: His sentiments concerning the last occupant of the bed, Hugh E. (Blazes) Boylan?

They place BLOOM in bed, his head on pillow at MOLLY'S feet.

ACTRESS A: More abnegation than jealousy.

ACTRESS C: Less envy than equanimity.

ACTRESS A: Then?

Sleepily BLOOM lifts MOLLY'S nightdress to kiss both buttocks.

ACTRESS D: He kissed the mellow melons of his wife's rump, on each plump melonous hemisphere.

ACTRESS B: What followed his silent action?

MOLLY rises on one elbow to look at BLOOM.

SAILOR: Catechetical interrogation.

VETERAN: Were there omissions in the narrator's reply?

ACTRESS A: The clandestine correspondence of Martha Clifford, one public altercation, the erotic provocation of Gertrude (Gerty), surname unknown.

KEEPER: Which person emerged as the salient point of his narration?

SAILOR: Stephen Dedalus, professor and author.

BLOOM settles to sleep, hand resting on nose. CAST retreat.

VETERAN: The childman weary, the manchild in the womb?

ACTRESS A: He rests. He has travelled.

ACTRESS C: With?

THE OTHERS: Sinbad the Sailor and Tinbad the Tailor and Jinbad the Jailor and Whinbad the Whaler and Rinbad the Railer and Dinbad the Kailer and Xinbad the Phthailer.

ACTRESS C: When?

THE OTHERS: Going to a dark bed there was a square round Sinbad the Sailor roc's auk's egg in the night of the bed of all the auks of the rocs of Darkinad the Brightdayler.

ACTRESS C: Where?

Blackout occurs on word.

SCENE SEVEN

Penelope. Molly's bedroom,   **2 a.m. (17th June)**

CAST have vanished. Spotlight finds MOLLY sitting up in bed.

MOLLY: (*Annoyed glance*)   O move over your big carcass out of that for the love of Mike - listen to him - well he may sleep if he knew how he came out on the cards this morning hed have something to sigh for - and Im to be slooching around in the kitchen to get his lordship his breakfast - will I indeed - show them attention and they treat you like dirt I dont care what anybody says itd be much better for the world to be governed by woman - when do you ever see woman rolling around drunk or losing every penny on horses - yes because a woman knows where to stop

yes I think he made them a bit firmer sucking them like that - titties he calls them - yes - they so beautiful of course compared with what a man looks like with his two bags full and his other thing hanging down or sticking up at you like a hatrack - what supposing I risked having another - not off him - I dont know - Poldy has more spunk in him yes

such an idea for him - bringing in his friends to entertain them - especially Simon Dedalus son - his father such a criticier - imagine climbing over the railings - wonder he didnt tear a big hole in his grand funeral trousers as if the one nature gave wasnt enough - hawking him down into the dirty old kitchen - is he right in his head sweet God when Im stretched out dead I suppose Ill have some peace - I want to get up a minute O Jesus - wait yes that thing has come on me - yes now wouldn't that affix you - of course all the poking and rooting he had up in me - now what am I to do - Friday Saturday Sunday - unless he likes it some men do - God knows theres always something wrong with us - usual monthly auction - I bet the cat itself is better off - O patience above its pouring out of me - anyhow he didnt make me pregnant as big as he is - I dont want to ruin the clean sheets - damn it damn it

She begins to rise from bed.

O Jamesy let me up out of this - pooh sweets of sin whoever suggested that business for women - what between cooking and children - this dammed old bed too jingling like the dickens till I suggested to put the quilt on the floor with the pillow under my bottom

Roots under bed for chamber pot.

wheres the chamber gone easy - Ive a holy horror of its breaking under me - wonder was I too heavy sitting on his knee - O this nuisance of a thing - (*Bells in background*) wait theres Georges church bells wait - 2 o clock well - thats a nice hour for him to be coming home at - Ill knock him off that little habit tomorrow - first Ill see if he has that French letter still in his pocketbook - I suppose he thinks I dont know

I wonder what sort is Dedalus son - he says hes an author and going to be a professor of Italian - what is he driving at now showing him my photo - I wonder he didnt make him a present of it altogether and me too - I saw him with his father and mother I was in mourning thats 11 years ago now yes Rudyd be 11 - I suppose hes a man now - I wonder is he too young - Im not too old for him - I hope hes not that stuck up university student sort no otherwise he wouldn't go sitting down in the kitchen taking cocoa - I'm sure he's very distinguished - Id like to meet a man like that - like that lovely little statue he bought - I often felt I wanted to kiss him all over - I wouldn't mind taking him im my mouth as if it was asking you to suck it - so clean and white he looked with his boyish face - I would too even if some of it went down - besides hed be so clean compared with those pigs of men I suppose never dream of washing it - thats what gives the woman the moustaches

itll be grand if I can only get in with a handsome young poet at my age - O but then what am I going to do about Boylan though - no he has no manners nor no refinement - the ignoramus that doesn't know poetry from a cabbage - thats what you get for not keeping them in their proper place

its a wonder Im not an old hag living with him - never embracing me except sometimes when hes asleep - the wrong end of me - any man thatd kiss a womans bottom Id throw my hat at - I suppose there isn't in all creation another man with the habits he has - nobody understands his cracked ideas but me

sure they wouldnt be in the world only for us - where would they be if they hadnt all a mother to look after them - thats why I suppose hes running wild now out all night - its a poor case that those that have a fine son theyre not satisfied and I none - I suppose I oughtnt to have buried him in that woolly jacket I knitted crying but give it to some poor child but I knew Id never have another - our 1st death too - we were never the same since - O Im not going to think myself into the glooms about that any more - I wonder why he wouldnt stay the night instead of roving around the city meeting God knows who - his poor mother wouldnt like that if she was alive

Ill just give him one more chance - Ill get up early - then Ill throw him up his eggs and tea - Ill go about rather gay and then Ill start dressing myself to go out - Ill put on my best shift and drawers - let him have a good eyeful to make his micky stand - Ill let him know if thats what he wanted that his wife is fucked yes and damn well fucked too - Ive a mind to tell him every scrap - serve him right - its all his fault if I am an adulteress - O much about it if thats all the harm ever we did in this vale of tears - God knows doesnt everybody only they hide it - I suppose thats what a woman is supposed to be there for or He wouldnt have made us so attractive

then if he wants to kiss my bottom Ill drag open my drawers and bulge it right out in his face - he can stick his tongue 7 miles up my hole as hes there - then Ill tell him I want 30 shillings to buy underclothes - Ill tighten my bottom well and let out a few smutty words - smellrump or lick my shit - than Ill suggest - O wait now but I was forgetting this bloody pest of a thing - pooh - you wouldn't know which to laugh or cry - What an unearthly hour I suppose theyre just getting up in China now - combing out their pigtails - well soon have the nuns ringing the angelus - theyve nobody coming in to spoil their sleep

better lower this lamp and try again - so I can get up early and get flowers to put about the place in case he brings him home tomorrow - today - whatll I wear - shall I wear a white rose - I love flowers - Id love to have the whole place swimming in roses - God theres nothing like nature - the wild mountains then the sea and the waves rushing - and flowers - all sorts of shapes and colours springing up even out in the ditches

the sun shines for you he said the day we were lying among the rhododendrons on Howth head - the day I got him to propose to me - yes - first I gave him the bit of seedcake out of my mouth - my God after that long kiss I near lost my breath - yes - he said I was a flower of the mountain - yes - so we are flowers - all a womans body - yes - that was why I liked him because I saw he understood or felt what a woman is - and I knew I could always get round him and I gave him all the pleasure I could - leading him on till he asked me to say yes - and I wouldnt answer first - only looked out over the sea and the sky - I was thinking of so many things he didnt know of - the sailors playing on the pier and the sentry in front of the governors house with the thing round his white helmet - and the Spanish girls laughing in their shawls and their tall combs and the auctions in the morning - the Greeks and the jews and the Arabs and the devil knows who else -

and the fowl market and the poor donkeys slipping half asleep - and the vague fellows in the cloaks asleep in the shade - and the old castle thousands of years old - yes - and those handsome Moors all in white and turbans like kings asking you to sit down in their little bit of a shop - and the wineshops half open at night - and the night we missed the boat at Algeciras - the watchman going about serene with his lamp and O that awful deep-down torrent - O and the sea the sea crimson sometimes like fire and the glorious sunsets - yes - and all the queer little streets and pink and blue and yellow houses and the rose gardens and the jessamine and geraniums - and Gilraltar as a girl where I was a flower of the mountain - yes when I put the rose in my hair like the Andalusian girls used - or shall I wear a red - yes - and how he kissed me under the Moorish wall - and I thought well as well him as another - and then I asked him with my eyes to ask again - yes - and then he asked me would I yes - to say yes - my mountain flower - and first I put my arms around him - yes and drew him down to me so he could feel my breasts all perfume - yes and his heart was going like mad - and yes I said yes I will Yes.

Light closes in around her.

The End

Dermot Bolger was born in Dublin in 1959. His often controversial novels of Irish life, *Night Shift*, *The Woman's Daughter*, *The Journey Home*, *Emily's Shoes* and *A Second Life* (all published by Penguin) have received such awards as The Macualay Fellowship and A.E. Memorial Prize and been translated into several European languages. His plays, *The Lament for Arthur Cleary*, *One Last White Horse*, *In High Germany* and *The Holy Ground* (published together by Penguin as *A Dublin Quartet*) have been presented in Ireland, Britain, Australia, America and Europe, broadcast on radio and television, and received such prizes as The Samuel Beckett Award, The Stewart Parker BBC Prize and an Edinburgh Fringe First Award. His latest play, *April Bright*, is presented by The Abbey Theatre on their Peacock stage, in August, 1995.

A poet and publisher, he is the editor of *The Picador Book of Contemporary Irish Fiction* among many other anthologies.